D0517509

DIESEL ENGINE

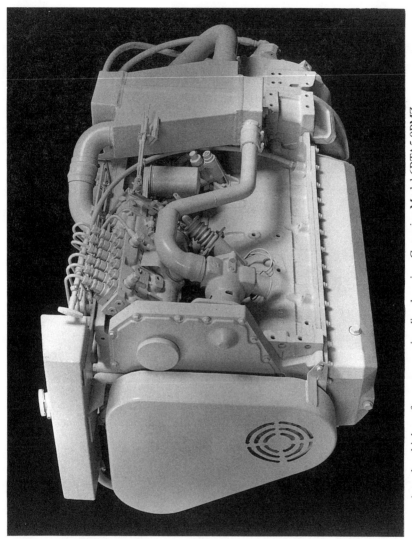

A modern high-performance marine diesel engine, Cummins Model 6BTA5.9PMZ (Courtesy Cummins Engine Co., Inc.)

DIESEL ENGINES

A Boat Owner's Guide
to Operation & Maintenance

LEO BLOCK, P.E.

CORNELL MARITIME PRESS
Centreville, Maryland

To the United States Navy, where I first learned
about diesel engines and where
I learned how to learn.

Copyright © 1991 by Cornell Maritime Press, Inc.

All rights reserved. No part of this book may be used or reproduced in any manner what-
soever without written permission except in the case of brief quotations embodied in
critical articles or reviews. For information, address Cornell Maritime Press, Inc.,
Centreville, Maryland 21617

Library of Congress Cataloging-in-Publication Data

Block, Leo, 1920–
    Diesel engines : a boat owner's guide to operation & maintenance /
by Leo Block.—1st ed.
        p.   c.m.
    Includes index.
    ISBN 0-87033-418-2 (paper) :
    1. Marine diesel motors—Handbooks, manuals, etc.   I. Title.
VM770.B564   1991
623.87'2368—dc20   90-55449
                                                                        CIP

Manufactured in the United States of America
First edition, 1991; third printing, 2001

Contents

Preface

THIS book differs from other current books on the subject of diesel engines for small craft in that it does not delve into the repair and overhaul of the basic engine. Instead, the text is devoted to describing proper engine operation and itemizing the maintenance tasks required to minimize the need for costly repair and overhaul. Also, the fundamental principles of operation are described in nontechnical terms, and safety precautions are explained and stressed.

Most boat owners do not have the time, tools, special equipment, or spare parts required for a major repair or overhaul of their boat's engine. Repair and adjustment of the fuel injection pump, injectors, and governor should not be attempted by even an experienced diesel mechanic; this work requires special tools and equipment, and is best performed by factory-trained personnel. Overhaul of the basic engine, with few exceptions, requires removal of the engine from the boat, a formidable task.

It is feasible for a boat owner to remove components, such as pumps, starter, and alternator, and replace them with repaired or new components. But major repair and overhaul should be performed in a reputable engine repair shop that is equipped with the special tools and fixtures required for the overhaul of the engine in question (special tools are usually required for the removal of injectors, cylinder liners, valve seats, etc.). Only then will the boat owner end up with an overhauled engine that will provide many years of satisfactory service.

However, the boat owner need not be an experienced mechanic to perform the routine maintenance on an engine. Special tools are not required. The explanation of the basic engine systems and the routine maintenance tasks presented in this text, augmented by the diesel engine manufacturer's manual, makes the execution of the maintenance tasks well within the capability of even a nontechnical boat owner.

Therefore, this book is for the boat owner who is interested in learning the fundamental concepts of diesel engines without delving into fundamental thermodynamic theory and who desires to minimize repairs and overhaul by proper operation and maintenance.

DIESEL ENGINES

Introduction

B efore you start working on a diesel engine, go wash your hands."
These were the words of my first diesel engine course instructor
many years ago. Since that time diesel engines have changed—
they are lighter, more powerful, and more efficient—but the requirement
for cleanliness has not changed. The need for clean air, clean fuel, and
clean lubricating oil cannot be overstressed. Most bearing failures are
caused by dirt in the lubricating oil originally introduced with the air
required for combustion. Most fuel injection pump and injector failures
are caused by impurities in the fuel.

All filter changes and other maintenance procedures must be performed with clean hands, clean tools, and clean materials, on an engine
that has been wiped clean to prevent the entry of foreign matter during
the servicing.

The engine manufacturer's manual must be studied for detailed
instructions. The intervals for filter changes and the frequency of other
maintenance tasks presented in this book are to be regarded as general
guidelines and are not meant to supersede instructions specified in the
manufacturer's manual.

CHAPTER 1

The Heat Engine

EARLY DEVELOPMENT

IN 1769 James Watt (1736–1819), a Scottish engineer, combined man's ability to control fire with his invention of the wheel, to create the steam engine.* This signalled the start of the Industrial Revolution, as man was no longer limited to work produced by beasts of burden and the strength of his own muscles. A steam engine actually consists of two major components: (1) the steam generator or boiler and (2) the engine, where steam pressure is converted into useful work (Fig. 1-1).

The boiler of Figure 1 consists of (1) a combustion chamber, in which fuel is burned in the presence of air, (2) tubes through which the hot gases flow on their way to the atmosphere, and (3) a drum that contains the water that surrounds the combustion chamber and tubes. Heat from the hot combustion products is transferred to the water, converting the water into steam. The steam, under pressure, is collected in the steam dome and is then piped to the engine.

The engine of Figure 1 consists of a cylinder with a pressure-tight plate at each end; a piston is located within the cylinder, and a rod, which protrudes through a hole in the bottom plate, is attached to the bottom of the piston. A slide valve is connected to openings at the top and bottom of the cylinder.

The slide valve allows steam to flow into the top of the cylinder to force the piston downward. The slide valve also allows the steam from the bottom of the cylinder to flow into the atmosphere. As the piston moves down, the slide valve moves upward and, at its approximate midposition, shuts off the supply of steam to the top of the cylinder. The steam above the piston then expands and continues to push the piston

---

*Actually, James Watt improved the steam-actuated pump invented by Newcomen and Calley (1712) but this improvement was of such importance that he is popularly credited with the invention of the steam engine.

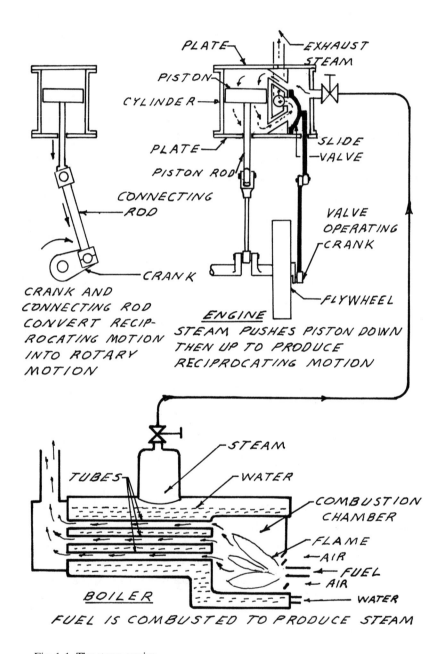

Fig. 1-1. The steam engine

downward. When the piston reaches its lowest position, the slide valve is in its upper position and it then supplies steam pressure to the bottom of the cylinder (forcing the piston upward) and allows the steam above the piston (now expanded to a low pressure) to be exhausted into the atmosphere. In this manner, steam pressure is converted into reciprocating (back-and-forth) motion.

By means of a connecting rod and crank, the up-and-down motion of the rod is converted into a rotary motion of the center shaft of the crank. When the rod moves downward, this motion is transmitted to the connecting rod by means of a bearing arrangement that permits a wristlike motion. The lower end of the rod, through its bearing, forces the outward end of the crank arm downward and imparts a rotary motion to the center shaft.

After the piston, rod, connecting rod, and crank arm attain their lowest position (bottom dead center), the upward movement of the piston transmits motion in like manner to rotate the center shaft in the same direction.

Useful work is obtained from the energy in the fuel by (1) combustion of fuel, (2) the formation of steam that drives a piston, and (3) use of a crank to convert reciprocating motion into rotary motion. Figure 1-1 shows a double-action engine—steam acts on both sides of the piston. Today's small craft diesel and gasoline engines are single action—gas pressure acts on only the top of the piston.

Although the early reciprocating engine required the use of many heavy moving parts and the boilers were extremely weighty due to the amount of water they contained, this combination was successfully used for over 100 years for ships, railroad trains, and stationary applications. Later some space and weight reductions were attained by the development of the turbine engine (in which rotational motion is obtained directly) and the use of small-diameter water tubes in the boiler. However, this improvement was still too bulky and heavy for widespread use on small boats and vehicles and there remained a need for a lightweight, compact heat engine.

INTERNAL COMBUSTION

In 1860, Jean Lenoir (1822–1900) managed to eliminate the need for a boiler by successfully combusting the fuel in the cylinder immediately above the piston when the piston was in its upper position. A combustion process requires fuel, oxygen (usually obtained from the air), and a momentary high temperature to ignite the fuel-air mixture; the process results in the formation of carbon dioxide, carbon monoxide, water vapor, and, mostly, nitrogen (these gasses are referred to as combustion products). Also, the combustion process releases a tremendous amount of heat. Gasses, when heated, expand if there is room for them to do so; if not, they experience an increase in pressure. In the internal combustion engine, the high gas pressure resulting from combustion of the fuel forces the piston downward in the same manner that the steam under pressure in a steam engine forces the piston downward. Elimination of the boiler resulted in the much-desired lightweight, compact heat engine. As the combustion of the fuel takes place within the cylinder, this type of heat engine is called an internal combustion engine.

Spark Ignition

A German engineer, Nikolaus A. Otto (1832–1891), improved the Lenoir engine to create today's widely used "spark ignition" gasoline engine. In this type of engine, fuel is first mixed with the air and this fuel-air mixture is admitted into the cylinder. Upward movement of the piston compresses the fuel-air mixture to about 80–125 psi. When the piston is at its top position, the compressed fuel-air mixture is ignited, by means of a spark, to immediately create a higher pressure that forces the piston in a downward direction.

Compression Ignition

A "compression ignition" engine was patented in England in 1888 and also in Germany in 1892 by the physicist Rudolf Diesel (1858–1913). In this engine, air only is admitted to the cylinder and compressed by the upward movement of the piston to a pressure of over 500 psi and consequently to a temperature of about 1,000°F. Fuel is then injected into the space above the piston and is ignited by the high-temperature air. This produces a much higher pressure than is available in the spark ignition engine and forces the piston downward.

Diesel's early engines were fueled by coal dust; this proved to be impractical and was abandoned in favor of fuel oil. At the beginning of the twentieth century Diesel's engines produced about 25 horsepower for each 10-inch-diameter cylinder and operated at 200 RPM.

In order to withstand the high pressures associated with compression ignition, the diesel engine is traditionally constructed of heavier and bulkier parts than the spark ignition engine. However, the diesel engine has the following advantages.

1. Better fuel economy.
2. No need for an electrical ignition system to provide a spark. This is particularly significant in marine applications where moisture-laden air can cause malfunction of the electrical ignition system.
3. Use of a safer fuel. Diesel fuel is much less volatile than gasoline which, given the opportunity, will vaporize to form heavier-than-air explosive vapors that tend to collect in the bilges.
4. Longer life (more operating hours between overhauls). In gasoline engines there is a tendency for the gasoline to contaminate the lubricating oil; this causes a loss in lubricity that accelerates the wear of moving parts.

In recent years, primarily due to the use of improved materials, the weight of diesel engines has been reduced substantially and the current trend is to equip even small boats with diesels. Sailboats of 27 feet and over are now almost exclusively equipped with diesel engines and fishing boats as small as 26 feet are diesel powered. Larger boats (over 30–35 feet), power and sail, have been diesel powered for several years. Only small, high-speed powerboats (23–32 feet) and outboards are commonly powered by spark ignition engines.

Four-Stroke Cycle
Most small diesel engines are of the four-stroke type. A stroke is the movement of the piston in an upward or downward direction; thus, there are two strokes for every revolution of the crankshaft. Four strokes are required for each power stroke, or movement of the piston downward to perform useful work. The strokes are identified as follows (Fig. 1-2).

1. Inlet Stroke. The inlet valve remains open while the piston moves downward, from its topmost position, and sucks air into the cylinder.
2. Compression Stroke. When the piston reaches its lowest position, the inlet valve closes (the exhaust valve is already closed) and the upward movement of the piston compresses the air trapped in the cylinder.
3. Power Stroke. When the piston is at the top of its stroke, fuel is injected into the space above the piston (the combustion chamber) and is ignited by the high-temperature compressed air. Combustion of the fuel results in a higher pressure that forces the piston downward and useful work is performed.

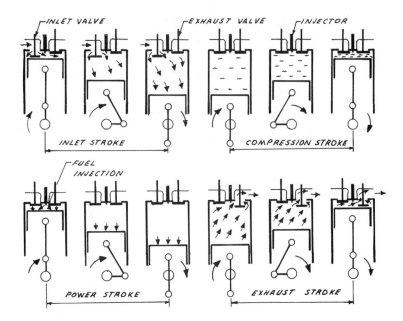

Fig. 1-2. The four-stroke cycle

4. Exhaust Stroke. When the pressure of the combustion products forces the piston to its lowest position, the exhaust valve opens and the upward movement of the piston forces the expended combustion products through the exhaust valve. The exhaust valve closes just before the piston again starts downward to repeat the cycle.

It is important to note that only one of four strokes produces useful work; the other three strokes merely prepare that cylinder for the all-important power stroke. A single-cylinder, four-stroke-cycle engine operating at 2,000 RPM will have 1,000 power strokes per minute. A two-cylinder engine will have 2,000 and a four-cylinder engine will have 4,000 power strokes per minute.

Two-Stroke Cycle
In the two-stroke-cycle engine only two strokes are required for each power stroke. Air under slight pressure is used to blow out the expended combustion products and to charge the cylinder with clean air. This process is called scavenging and a scavenging air blower (Roots type),

driven by the engine crankshaft, is used to pressurize the air. Most two-stroke-cycle diesel engines have scavenging air inlet openings at the bottom of the cylinder and two exhaust valves at the top of the cylinder. The operating cycle is as follows (Fig. 1-3).

1. Scavenging and Compression Stroke. When the piston is in its lower position, the exhaust valves are open and the scavenging air ports are uncovered; scavenging air flows into the bottom of the cylinder and displaces the spent combustion products.

   When the piston moves upward to close off the scavenging air ports, the exhaust valves also close, trapping the air in the cylinder.

   Further movement of the piston in the upward direction compresses the air to about 1/20 of its original volume (compression ratio of 20:1).

2. Power and Scavenging Stroke. When the piston is at the top of its stroke, fuel is injected; the resulting combustion creates a high pressure to force the piston downward and useful work is performed.

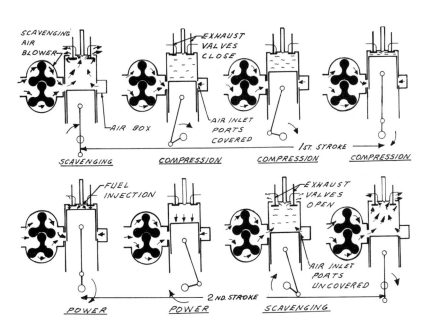

Fig. 1-3. The two-stroke cycle

As the piston approaches its lower position, the exhaust valves open and the scavenging air ports are uncovered by the piston and the scavenging process commences.

In the two-stroke-cycle engine, there is a power stroke for each revolution; a single-cylinder engine operating at 2,000 RPM would have 2,000 power strokes per minute and a two-cylinder engine would have 4,000 power strokes per minute. Because of the greater number of power strokes, these engines tend to produce more horsepower than a four-stroke-cycle engine of comparable size. However, the two-stroke engine is noisier than the four-stroke because exhaust gasses are released at a higher pressure. The four-stroke engine usually has better fuel economy.

The description of four- and two-stroke-cycle operation is also valid for spark ignition engines except that a fuel-air mixture instead of air only is admitted to the cylinder, and combustion is instigated by means of a spark.

CLASSIFICATION OF HEAT ENGINES

Figure 1-4 is a chart showing the classification of heat engines. Heat engines are sometimes referred to as motors; however, a device that burns fuel to create heat to perform work is a heat engine, or engine for short. A motor converts one form of energy into useful work without the intentional generation of heat and without burning fuel.

The Sterling engine is similar in operation to a steam engine except that hot air is the medium instead of steam; in spite of its high efficiency, the Sterling engine never became popular because of its tremendous bulk. Gas turbines and jet engines can theoretically be classified as external combustion engines because their combustion chamber is separate from the area where the energy of the gas is converted into useful work; however, under certain conditions combustion may take place in the work conversion area.

ENGINE SYSTEMS

For an internal combustion engine to provide the all-important power stroke reliably and efficiently, the following support systems are required:

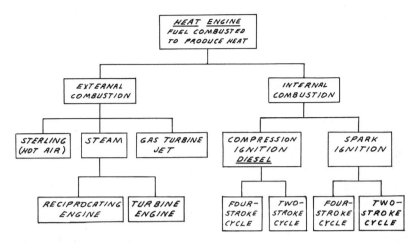

Fig. 1-4. Classification of heat engines

- Water cooling
- Lubricating oil
- Combustion air
- Fuel
- Exhaust
- Starting
- Power transmission

These systems and related subjects will be described in subsequent chapters, but first it is necessary to define the major components of the engine.

CHAPTER 2

Major Engine Components

FIGURE 2-1 shows the major components of a diesel engine. The main structural member of most diesel engines is the *cylinder block* (Fig. 2-2). This is usually a cast metal part that includes circular openings (accurately machined *cylinders*) and a cooling water passage (jacket) around each cylinder. The bottom of the cylinder block forms the *crankcase*. The *oil sump* is attached to the bottom of the crankcase. On some engines the oil sump is the main structural member and individual cylinders are attached to it.

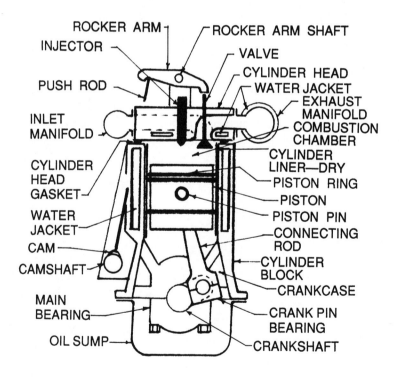

Fig. 2-1. Major engine components

Fig. 2-2. Cylinder block (Courtesy Caterpillar Inc.)

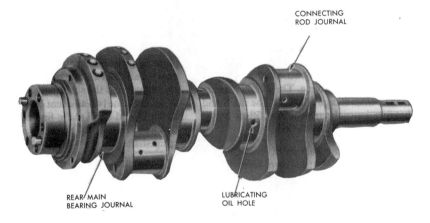

CONNECTING
ROD JOURNAL

REAR MAIN
BEARING JOURNAL

LUBRICATING
OIL HOLE

Fig. 2-3. Crankshaft (Courtesy Detroit Diesel Corp.)

The *main bearings* position the *crankshaft* (Fig. 2-3) within the crankcase and include *bearing shells* (Fig. 2-4) that can be replaced when worn.

Cylinder liners (Fig. 2-5) are pressed into the cylinders of the cylinder block to permit replacement when worn. Cylinder liners are of two types, dry and wet. Dry liners do not come in contact with the

Fig. 2-4. Main bearing shells (Courtesy Detroit Diesel Corp.)

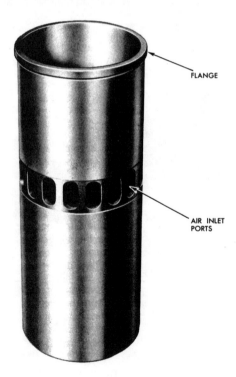

Fig. 2-5. Cylinder liner—two cycle (Courtesy Detroit Diesel Corp.)

cooling water (Fig. 2-1); wet liners are equipped with gaskets, and the cooling water flows around the outer surface of the wet liner.

The piston fits into the cylinder liner and is fitted with *piston rings* (Fig. 2-6) to minimize leakage between the piston and the wall of the cylinder liner. The *piston pin* (Fig. 2-6) attaches the piston to the upper end of the *connecting rod* (Fig. 2-7) and permits the wristlike motion between the piston and the connecting rod. The lower end of the connecting rod includes a crankpin bearing to permit attachment to the crankpin of the crankshaft. The crankpin bearing is also equipped with bearing shells that can be replaced when worn. The piston pin, connecting rod, and crankshaft convert the reciprocating motion of the piston into rotary motion of the center of the crankshaft.

The *cylinder head* (Fig. 2-8) includes water cooling passages and is attached to the top of the cylinder block by means of threaded studs and nuts. A *cylinder head gasket* is used to make a gas-tight joint. Cooling water from the cylinder block flows upward through holes in the gasket and into the cylinder head (Fig. 2-9).

The cylinder head of a four-stroke-cycle engine is equipped with *inlet* and *exhaust valves* (Fig. 1-2). A two-stroke-cycle engine is usually equipped with two exhaust valves; the inlet valve function is performed by the air inlet port and the piston (Fig. 1-3). An *air inlet manifold* and an *exhaust manifold* (with water passages for cooling) are attached to the

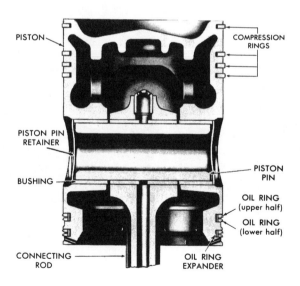

Fig. 2-6. Piston, piston pin, and piston rings (Courtesy Detroit Diesel Corp.)

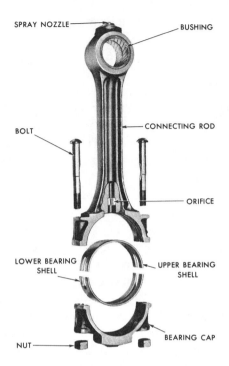

Fig. 2-7. Connecting rod and crankpin bearing (Courtesy Detroit Diesel Corp.)

Fig. 2-8. Cylinder head (Courtesy Detroit Diesel Corp.)

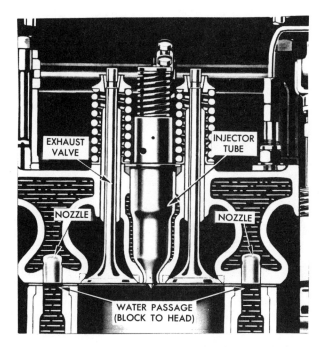

Fig. 2-9. Cooling water in upper cylinder block and cylinder head (Courtesy Detroit Diesel Corp.)

cylinder head. Each valve is actuated by a *rocker arm* that pivots about a *rocker arm shaft.* A *camshaft,* usually located at the side of the cylinder block, actuates the rocker arm by means of a *pushrod.* On some engines the camshaft is located on top of the cylinder head and directly actuates the rocker arm (overhead cam arrangement).

When actuated by the pushrod, or directly by an overhead camshaft, the opposite end of the rocker arm forces the valve stem downward, compressing the *valve spring* and moving the valve face away from the valve seat (Fig. 2-10). The valve is now open. After the camshaft rotates so that the cam is no longer engaged, the compressed valve spring forces the face against the seat to close the valve.

The *gear train* (Fig. 2-11), usually located at the front of the engine, consists of a gear attached to the crankshaft and other gears that drive the camshaft and fuel pump. The *flywheel* (Fig. 2-12) is usually located at the opposite end of the engine; the weight of the flywheel provides the momentum to rotate the crankshaft from one power stroke

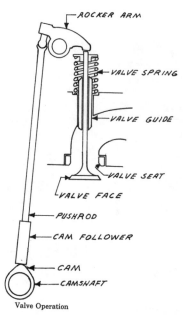

Fig. 2-10. Valve operation

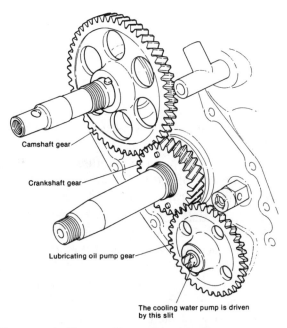

Fig. 2-11. The gear train (Courtesy Yanmar Diesel Engine (USA), Inc.)

Fig. 2-12. Flywheel detached from crankshaft (Courtesy Caterpillar Inc.)

to the next power stroke. A *ring gear* is attached to the outer periphery of the flywheel; the *pinion gear* of the *starter motor* engages the ring gear to rotate the engine for starting. A *generator* or *alternator* is belt driven from the crankshaft to recharge the battery that supplies electric power for starting and for other electrical equipment.

A *transmission* (or gearbox) is attached to (usually) the flywheel end of the crankshaft to permit manual shifting of the *propeller* from AHEAD to NEUTRAL to REVERSE (Fig. 2-13). Some transmissions are equipped with a *reduction gear* to permit the propeller to rotate at a speed slower than the engine speed (a lower propeller speed is usually more efficient).

The V-belt has a V-shaped cross section and is made of a flexible material. It is readily accessible at the forward end of the engine and is used to drive the generator or alternator; it may also be used to drive a water pump and other auxiliary equipment (e.g., refrigeration compressor, bilge pump).

Isolation mounts provide a resilient attachment of the engine to the hull structure. Usually they include an adjustable means to permit alignment of the engine to the propeller shaft.

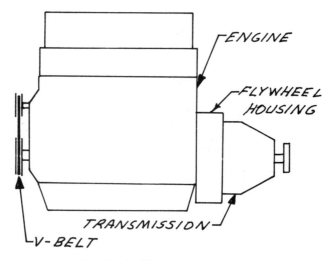

Fig. 2-13. Transmission attached to flywheel housing

The engine is also equipped with components that are included in the various engine systems. These components are identified and discussed in subsequent chapters.

CHAPTER 3

The Water Cooling System

IN today's diesel engine, about one-third of the heat released during combustion is converted into useful work; another one-third, approximately, is discharged with the exhaust gasses; and the remainder is removed by the cooling system to prevent overheating of (and subsequent damage to) the engine. The engine is cooled by circulating water through passages in the (1) cylinder block (around the cylinders), (2) the cylinder head, and (3) the exhaust manifold. Air cooling has been used on diesel engines but not successfully for marine applications. Three basic types of liquid cooling systems are currently used for marine diesel engines:

1. Raw water cooling
2. Heat exchanger cooling
3. Keel cooling

RAW WATER COOLING

Shown in Figure 3-1, this is the simplest system because the water in which the vessel is floating is used to cool the engine. An engine-driven pump sucks the raw water through a sea cock and strainer and discharges it through the engine-cooling water passages and then overboard (usually with the engine exhaust). On most engines a thermostat is utilized to maintain a constant water temperature.

In seawater, the operating temperature of a raw water cooling system is usually limited to about 140°F; a higher temperature will hasten the formation of salt scale deposits that will impede the flow of cooling water, particularly in the hottest areas (adjacent to the combustion chambers and exhaust valves) where maximum cooling is required. Extensive scale buildup may result in a cracked head, usually in the vicinity of an exhaust valve. The optimum operating temperature for a diesel engine is 180–190°F. Thus, the raw water-cooled engine, operating in seawater, is forced to maintain an ab-

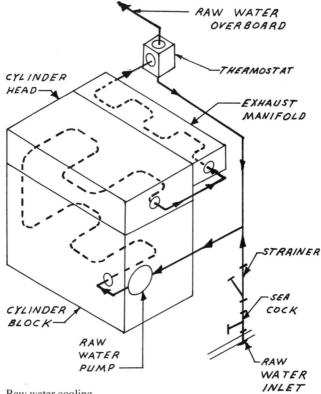

Fig. 3-1. Raw water cooling

normally low coolant temperature and this results in the following three disadvantages:

1. Water vapor from the combustion process tends to condense on the relatively cool cylinder walls and this moisture drains downward and contaminates the lubricating oil.
2. The combustion process is less complete because of the low temperature of the cylinder walls. This tends to accentuate the formation of carbon deposits and results in more soot in the exhaust. Also, unburned fuel tends to dilute the lubricating oil.
3. The thermostatic arrangement has difficulty maintaining a constant (140°F) temperature, particularly at extremely low raw water temperatures.

The raw water system has the following additional disadvantages:

4. Mud, sand, silt, and small particles of foreign matter that pass through the strainer have the opportunity to clog the thermostat and to settle in the pockets of the water passages, restricting the flow of cooling water.
5. Seawater, particularly, has a corrosive effect on the metal walls of the cooling water passages.

Raw water cooling systems are presently not used on high-speed, lightweight, high-performance engines but have been successfully used on heavier, slower-speed engines.

HEAT EXCHANGER COOLING

This system, shown in Figure 3-2, is similar to an automotive cooling system except that raw water, rather than air, is used to cool the fresh water circulated through the engine. Instead of an air-cooled radiator, a heat exchanger is used; raw water is pumped through tubes and absorbs heat from the fresh water that is circulated around the tubes. The raw water is then discharged overboard and the fresh water is circulated by a separate pump through the water passages. A thermostat arrangement maintains the cooling water temperature at 180–190°F as there is no danger of scale buildup. An antifreeze solution with corrosion inhibitors is commonly used in place of fresh water.

An expansion tank, with a pressure cap usually set at 10 psi, is located above the engine and provides improved cooling, as the higher water pressure (and corresponding higher boiling temperature) reduces the possibility of localized boiling at the hot spots.

The heat exchanger cooling system eliminates all of the disadvantages of the raw water system but requires an extra water pump, a heat exchanger, and an expansion tank with pressure cap. Current production high-speed, lightweight, high-performance diesel engines utilize the heat exchanger cooling system.

KEEL COOLING

Keel cooling shown in Figure 3-3 is a simplified version of the heat exchanger system; the fresh water is cooled by circulating it through a pipe (or pipes) located outside of the hull and parallel to the keel. Since

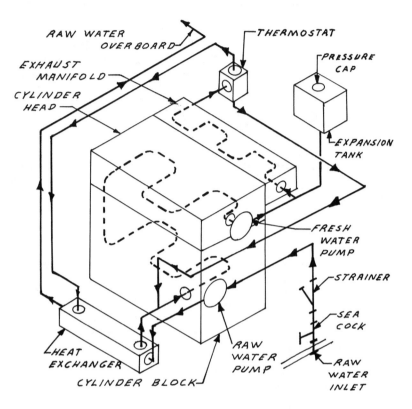

Fig. 3-2. Heat exchanger cooling

the fresh water transfers its heat directly to the water in which the vessel is floating, the heat exchanger, raw water pump, strainer, and sea cock are not required. This elimination of the raw water system is a substantial advantage; however, the external keel cooler piping requires periodic cleaning and is susceptible to damage in the event of grounding. An added disadvantage of keel cooling is the absence of raw water for cooling the engine exhaust.

OTHER COOLERS

Many of today's engines employ lubricating oil coolers, transmission oil coolers, and turbocharger after- or inner coolers. On a keel cooler installation, only fresh water is available to absorb heat in these coolers. On a

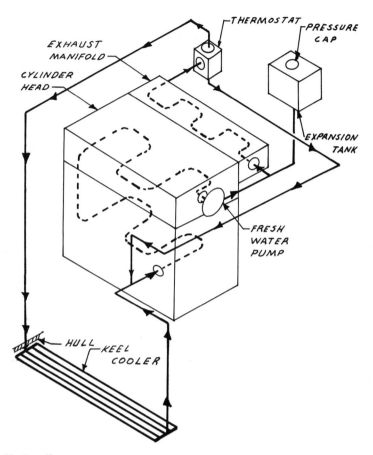

Fig. 3-3. Keel cooling

heat exchanger system some coolers may utilize fresh water and others raw water. Maximum cooling (for a given size cooler) is obtained by the use of raw water, as it is substantially colder than the fresh water, but corrosion problems accompany the use of raw water.

RAW WATER CIRCUIT MAINTENANCE

In raw water cooling and heat exchanger cooling systems, the following components require attention.

Sea Cock

The sea cock should be operated frequently to insure that it can be rapidly closed in the event of an emergency (e.g., a ruptured water hose). Best practice calls for closing the sea cock when the engine is not to be used for a period of time and especially when the vessel is unattended. The sea cock should be repaired or replaced if it is difficult to operate or if there is any evidence of corrosion.

When removing any raw water system component located below the waterline, the sea cock must obviously be closed. After reinstalling the component and opening the sea cock, it is important to bleed the high points; trapped air may prevent water circulation. The manufacturer's manual usually identifies the bleed points.

Strainer

A clogged strainer will result not only in an overheated engine but may cause the raw water pump impeller to burn out. The frequency of strainer inspection and cleaning is best established by experience, as it depends on the amount of seaweed, kelp, and other contaminants in the water.

All raw water systems should include a strainer. Unfortunately not all boatbuilders install strainers, but this is an inexpensive part to add. Caution: When installing a strainer, make sure that an air trap is not created. Water with entrained air should normally flow in an upward or horizontal direction. Downward flow will tend to allow air to accumulate at the high points and act as a flow-restricting baffle.

Raw Water Pump

The impeller of most raw water pumps is made of a rubberlike material with vanes that deflect (bend) as the impeller rotates (Fig. 3-4). Once each season the impeller should be removed and carefully examined for excessive wear, missing vanes, and cracks at the base of each vane; if any of these conditions exist, the impeller should be replaced. An impeller with one or two missing vanes (Fig. 3-5) can usually still be used (if a spare is not available), but it is imperative that the missing vanes be found. This may require disassembly of the discharge piping; the missing segment(s) may lodge in a fitting and reduce the flow of coolant or the vane may jam the thermostat element and prevent its operation.

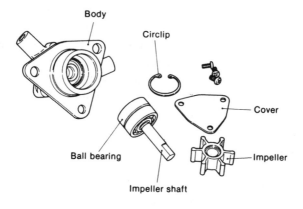

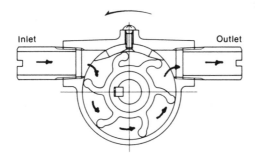

Fig. 3-4. Raw water pump (Courtesy Yanmar Diesel Engine (USA), Inc.)

Fig. 3-5. Raw water pump impeller with missing vane

Access to the impeller is obtained by removal of the pump end plate, but special snap ring pliers may be required to remove the snap ring that prevents the impeller from sliding off the end of the shaft. The impeller should be reinstalled so that it rotates in the same direction but the pump cavity should first be greased to facilitate installation of the impeller and to provide lubrication on first start-up (until water gets to it). The engine manufacturer's manual usually includes complete instructions for disassembly and reassembly. Most pumps have a leak-off hole located between the pump body and the cylinder block; water dripping from this hole indicates a defective seal that requires replacement. A spare impeller and end plate gasket should be kept on board.

Piston and diaphragm pumps have also been used for circulation of raw water. These pumps also require seasonal disassembly and inspection of the piston O-rings or diaphragm. Pumps of this type (reciprocating) are fitted with inlet and outlet check valves (which permit flow only in one direction) that should also be disassembled and inspected. If the rubberlike material shows signs of wear, pinholes, or cracking, the part should be replaced.

After disassembly or draining, the raw water pump may require priming (see manufacturer's manual) by removing the pipe plug in the pump outlet and pouring water into the pump.

Caution: Failure to prime the raw water pump may result in damage to the pump impeller.

Zincs

Raw water (particularly seawater) tends to corrode metal surfaces. When zincs are inserted into the raw water, most of the corrosive (galvanic) effect is directed towards the zinc, which gradually disintegrates. Thus, the zinc is sacrificed to protect other metal surfaces and requires periodic replacement.

Usually zincs that are used to protect raw water systems are attached to a pipe plug and are referred to as "pencil zincs," because they have the shape of a pencil (Fig. 3-6). These pencil zincs are commonly installed in heat exchangers, oil coolers, and cylinder blocks, but may be located anywhere in the raw water system. The manufacturer's manual usually specifies location. Each pencil zinc exposed to seawater should be removed (by unscrewing its pipe plug) for inspection at least once every two months and replaced if it crumbles when lightly tapped with a hammer or if it is pitted or significantly shortened.

FRESHWATER CIRCUIT MAINTENANCE

This type of system is used for heat exchanger and keel cooling and the following components require maintenance.

Freshwater Pump

This circulating pump (Fig. 3-7) is usually a belt-driven, ball bearing, automotive type centrifugal pump that normally requires no maintenance other than adjustment of the V-belt tension (Fig. 3-11). Once each season the belt should be removed and the water pump pulley rotated by hand to check for radial and axial movement of the shaft; excessive movement indicates defective bearings and the entire assembly should be removed and a new or repaired assembly reinstalled.

Most pumps have a drain hole between the pulley and the body of the pump. Water dripping from the drain hole indicates a defective seal that requires replacement.

Heat Exchanger

Normally heat exchangers require no service other than the replacement of the sacrificial pencil zincs; however, periodic inspection for foreign matter lodged in the tubes is recommended. Most heat exchangers (Fig. 3-8) and coolers have removable heads sealed with O-rings; after removal of the heads, the tubes can be flushed out with a water hose or may be cleaned by inserting a wooden dowel (metal may damage the tube walls).

Antifreeze Coolant

Instead of water, an antifreeze solution is recommended, because it performs the same cooling function as does water but also protects against

Fig. 3-6. Pencil zinc

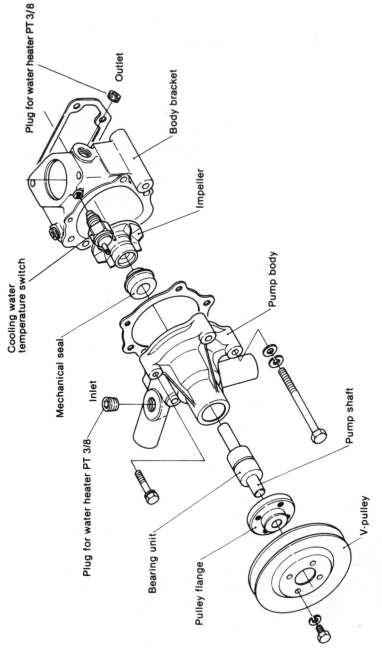

Fig. 3-7. Freshwater pump (Courtesy Yanmar Diesel Engine (USA), Inc.)

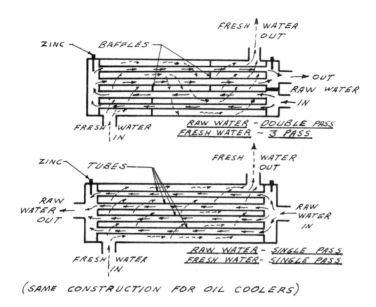

Fig. 3-8. Heat exchanger variations

winter freeze-up and corrosion of metal surfaces. Prior to each winter season, the coolant should be checked (density measurement with a hydrometer) to determine if additional antifreeze must be added to provide the required freeze protection. It is considered good practice to change the antifreeze solution every few years to insure that the rust-inhibiting chemicals have not been expended. If for any reason antifreeze solution is not available, only distilled water or soft water should be used and must be drained for winter lay-up to prevent freeze damage.

When refilling a freshwater cooling system, air must be vented at the high points (usually at the heat exchanger, oil cooler, and exhaust manifold); refer to the manufacturer's manual for location of the vent points. Unless otherwise specified by the manufacturer, the coolant level should be about $1/2$ to 1 inch below the top of the expansion tank. After filling, run the engine for a few minutes and again check the level; add coolant if necessary.

Pressure Cap

The pressure cap seals the coolant fill opening at the top of the expansion tank (Fig. 3-9). It includes a spring-loaded valve arrangement that per-

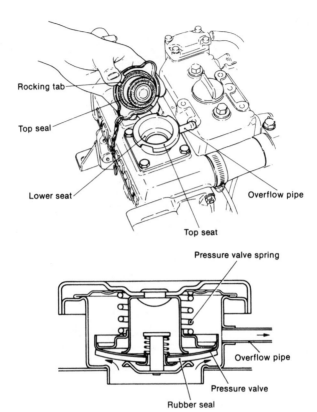

Rocking tab

Top seal

Lower seat

Top seat

Overflow pipe

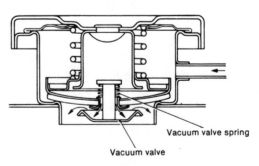

Pressure valve spring

Overflow pipe

Pressure valve

Rubber seal

Pressure valve operation

Vacuum valve spring

Vacuum valve

Vacuum valve operation

Fig. 3-9. Pressure cap (Courtesy Yanmar Diesel Engine (USA), Inc.)

mits the coolant to attain the pressure stamped on the cap. To check the pressure setting, the cap must be taken to an automotive repair shop. It should be replaced if the pressure setting is incorrect or if there is any evidence of coolant leakage about the cap.

Danger! Use extreme care when removing a pressure cap on a hot engine. The coolant is at a high temperature and is under pressure. When the pressure cap is loosened, this scalding fluid will tend to spray in all directions.

MAINTENANCE ON ALL SYSTEMS

Hoses and Clamps

Most engine failures are caused by overheating, and a common cause of overheating is leakage or failure of a cooling water hose. Hoses should be frequently (at least once each season) inspected and replaced if they show any evidence of brittleness, cracking, deforming, or swelling. Hoses for use on the suction side of a raw water pump must be of the noncollapsible type.

Two hose clamps should be used at each end of a hose and, if corroded, they should be replaced with stainless steel clamps (with a positive stainless steel worm gear tightening arrangement).

Freeze Plugs

These are soft metal discs that are pressed into the outside of the cylinder block at the bottom of the cooling water passage. They are designed to break out in the event of freeze-up to prevent cracking of the cylinder block (water expands when freezing). These plugs should be examined at least once each season and replaced if there is any evidence of leakage or seepage.

Thermostat

On freshwater systems the thermostat is usually located in the freshwater circuit and normally requires no maintenance unless the temperature gauge shows an abnormal reading. On raw water systems the thermostat should be inspected periodically to remove any accumulated foreign matter.

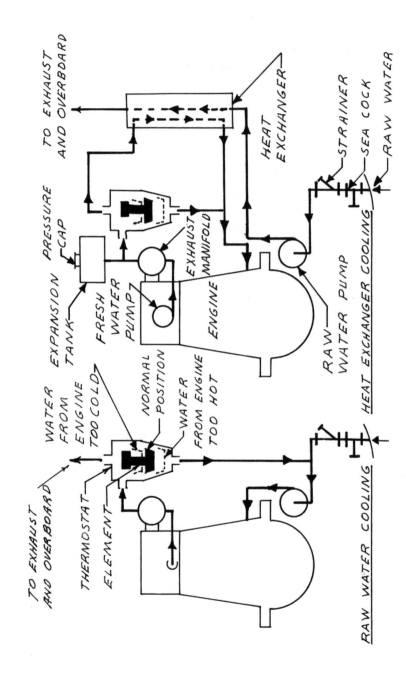

Fig. 3-10. The cooling system thermostat

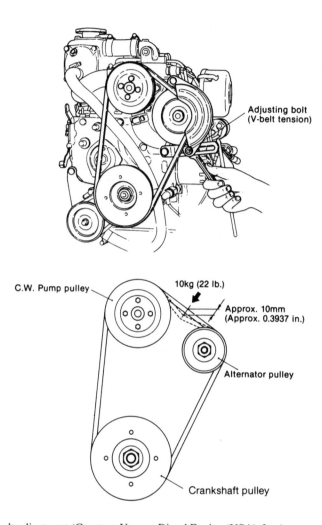

Adjusting bolt
(V-belt tension)

C.W. Pump pulley

10kg (22 lb.)

Approx. 10mm
(Approx. 0.3937 in.)

Alternator pulley

Crankshaft pulley

Fig. 3-11. V-belt adjustment (Courtesy Yanmar Diesel Engine (USA), Inc.)

Actually, the thermostat is a three-way valve that allows some of the heated water from the engine to be returned directly to the engine and the remaining water to flow through the heat exchanger, or overboard on raw water systems. A thermostatic element proportions the flow as necessary to maintain the desired engine outlet water temperature (Fig. 3-10). Usually the thermostat is located at the top of the engine; removing the fasteners and prying up the thermostat housing will provide access to the element, which can then be withdrawn from its cavity. To check for calibration, the element is placed into a pan of water that is gradually heated; a thermometer is required to monitor the water temperature. If the thermostatic element does not open at the temperature specified by the manufacturer, it should be replaced. A spare element and housing gasket should be carried on board.

V-Belt

At least once each season the V-belt should be removed, inspected, and replaced if there are any visible cracks or signs of wear. A spare belt should be carried on board. Belt tension is usually adjusted by means of the alternator pulley. Unless the manufacturer's manual specifies otherwise, the adjustment should permit a $1/2$-inch deflection when the belt is subjected to finger pressure (Fig. 3-11).

Danger! Keep hands, loose clothing, neckties, long hair, test leads, rags, etc., well away from a rotating belt to prevent the possibility of entanglement. Never operate an engine with guards, covers, or screens removed.

Winter Lay-Up

All cooling water systems must be drained (including low spots and cavities) or filled with antifreeze.

CHAPTER 4

The Lubricating Oil System

NOT all of the engine cooling is performed by the cooling system; a significant amount of heat (mostly from the piston, piston rings, and bearings) is absorbed by the lubricating oil that is circulated throughout the engine. The heat is then released in an oil cooler or, on small engines, is dissipated to the surrounding air when the oil is in the sump. The primary function of the lubricating oil is to reduce the friction of moving parts by providing a film cushion to minimize metal-to-metal contact. Oil also keeps the engine clean and rust free and acts as a sealant between the piston rings and the cylinder wall (minimizes blow-by).

The diesel engine lubrication system (Fig. 4-1) is similar to that of an automotive gasoline engine except that a different oil is required. Because of the higher pressures and temperatures in a diesel, the oil is usually fortified with the following additives:

1. Detergents to control formation of deposits by adhering to the contaminants and keeping them in suspension until they can be deposited in the filter.
2. Dispersants that bond themselves to contaminants so that the contaminants cannot bond to themselves and form sludge.
3. Alkalinity agents to help neutralize acids formed by sulphur in the fuel uniting with moisture from condensation.
4. Pour-point dispersants to inhibit wax formation.
5. Viscosity improvers to prevent thinning of oil at high temperatures.
6. Anti-wear agents to reduce friction.
7. Oxidation inhibitors to prevent buildup of viscosity.

Oil contaminants normally consist of the following:

1. Dirt entering with the combustion air.
2. Carbon from unburned fuel.

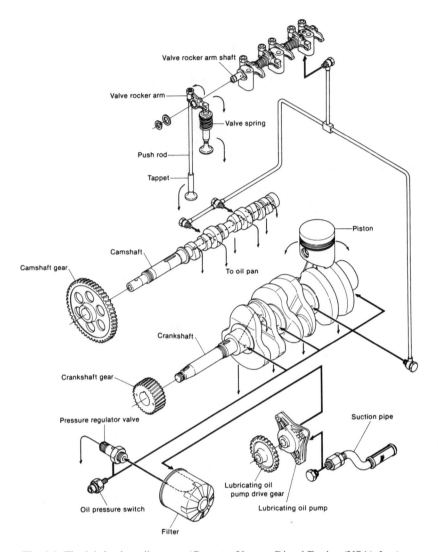

Fig. 4-1. The lubricating oil system (Courtesy Yanmar Diesel Engine (USA), Inc.)

3. Fuel (usually including sulphur) that leaks past the piston rings.
4. Metal particles from wear of the moving parts.
5. Water from a defective oil cooler or from condensation.
6. Antifreeze (ethylene glycol) due to a leaky head gasket or a cracked head or cylinder block.

Although oil additives prolong useful life, the contaminants force periodic oil changes, primarily to prevent acid buildup caused by the gradual accumulation of sulphur and moisture.

The manufacturer's manual specifies the API (American Petroleum Institute) classification of oil that should be used (usually CD or CE) and the proper viscosity (SAE 30, 10W/40, SAE 40, or 15W/40). A special oil is usually specified for break-in of a new engine. Oils formulated exclusively for use on gasoline engines are not suitable; however, some oils are formulated for use on both gasoline and diesel engines (SF, SG/CD, CE).

THE OIL PATH

Lubricating oil is stored in the sump (oil pan), which is usually located under the crankcase, and is circulated by a gear-driven oil pump. The pump is equipped with a strainer (on the suction side) and a relief valve (on the discharge side). Unless there is extreme sludge formation, the strainer requires no service; its function is to filter out any large foreign matter particles that somehow entered the oil sump. The spring-loaded relief valve limits the oil pressure to a safe level by allowing some of the oil to flow back to the sump; excessive oil pressure may result in oil leakage at shaft seals. The relief valve and oil sump require no service as long as the oil pressure gauge indicates the pressure specified by the manufacturer.

The oil then flows to a full-flow filter with a replaceable element and a bypass arrangement. If the element becomes clogged (due to non-replacement or an excess of water or other contaminants) the oil flows through the bypass to insure a full flow of oil to the engine. On some vessels that accumulate many more operating hours than the average recreational vessel, a bypass filter is installed in addition to the full-flow filter. Only a small percentage of the total flow passes through the by-pass filter (and is then returned to the sump) but much finer filtration is attained. The bypass filter extends the life of the oil by decreasing the contamination level.

After flowing through the oil cooler (omitted on small engines) the oil enters a distribution passage in the cylinder block (the oil gallery) from which most of the oil flows first to the main bearings, then through drilled passages in the crankshaft to the connecting rod bearings. After that, it flows through drilled passages in the connecting rods to the piston pins and is then sprayed against the underside of the pistons where some of the oil is diverted to the piston rings and cylinder walls. The oil then drains down through the crankcase and into the sump to complete the cycle. A small volume of oil is delivered directly to the camshaft bearings, rocker arms, valve stems, and the timing gear train. On turbocharged engines, oil is also delivered to the turbocharger bearing; some engines are equipped with a separate turbocharger oil filter.

LUBRICATING OIL ANALYSIS

A laboratory analysis of an engine's lubricating oil will reveal a surprisingly accurate evaluation of the condition of the engine. While the engine is operating, parts subjected to wear gradually deposit minute metal particles that are kept in suspension in the oil. The analysis process consists of identifying these particles and determining their concentration. The results are then compared with (1) specifications for that make and model of engine, (2) total operating hours on the engine since last overhaul, and (3) the operating hours on the oil tested. This permits establishment of wear trends that warn of impending failures and optimizes the scheduling of an overhaul.

In addition, an oil analysis program can detect fuel, water, and coolant leaks; clogged or malfunctioning filters; the presence of foreign substances; the presence and concentration of acid; the degradation of oil additives; and the total solids content. Some commercial operators rely on oil analysis, rather than operating hours, to determine when an oil change is required. Commercial fishermen rely on oil analysis to minimize the probability of breakdown at sea, but most recreational boaters have not yet adopted this practice.

Oil analysis is not complex or expensive. Analysts, Inc. (of Torrance, California) provide a sampling bellows that is both a sampler and a mailer. It includes a tube that is inserted into the oil sump to withdraw the sample. The tube is then discarded and the sampling bellows is mailed to one of Analysts' five laboratories. Results (Fig. 4-2) are obtained by return mail in about one week; the cost is about $25. Some fuel docks also provide oil analysis service.

MAINTENANCE

Oil Change

The frequency of oil change is specified in the manufacturer's manual (usually every 100 to 200 operating hours but at least once each season)

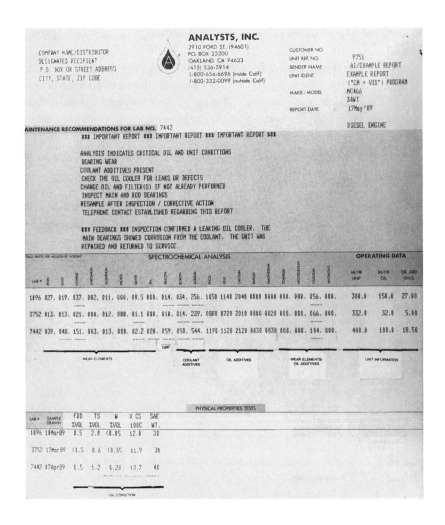

Fig. 4-2. Lubricating oil analysis report (Courtesy Analysts, Inc.)

and must not be extended. Before the lubricating oil is drained, the engine must be operated (under load) to insure that the engine is at its normal operating temperature. Then the engine is shut down and the oil drained while it is still hot. *Danger!* Keep hands out of the hot oil.

Unless the engine is equipped with a sump pump, oil drainage is usually difficult and messy. The oil sump drain plug is under the engine and often is not accessible. Even when it is possible to put a wrench on the drain plug, usually there is no room for a container to collect the drained oil. Some engines are equipped with a drain pan located under the engine to collect the oil, which is then removed with a hand-operated pump.

The usual method for removing oil when a sump pump is not fitted is to remove the dipstick and to insert a small-diameter suction hose of a hand pump into the dip tube. The oil is then pumped into a suitable container (Fig. 4-3). However, this is not the optimum method as not all of the oil is removed.

An improved method is to permanently attach a drain hose to the oil sump drain; most engine manufacturers offer an oil hose drain kit. To drain the oil, the plug is removed from the end of the hose and the open end is lowered to allow the oil to drain into a container, or the open end can be attached to a hand pump (Fig. 4-4). *Caution:* After draining, the plug must be reinstalled (and tightened, using two wrenches). As an added precaution, the end of the hose can be secured at a high level (above the level of the oil in the sump).

After oil drainage, the bilges and area surrounding the engine must be cleaned. U.S. Coast Guard regulations forbid any accumulation of oil in bilges and require that in every engine compartment a notice to this effect be posted (Fig. 4-5). These notices are available in most marine stores.

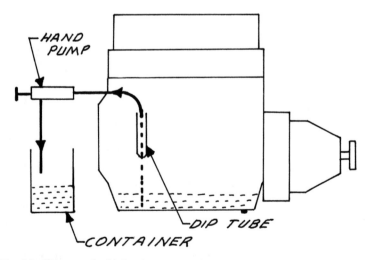

Fig. 4-3. Oil removal with hand pump

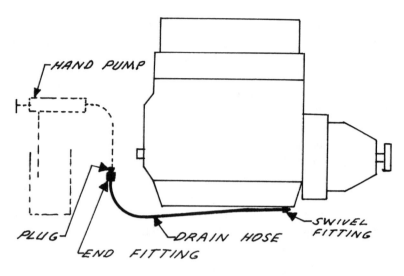

Fig. 4-4. Oil drain hose kit for oil removal

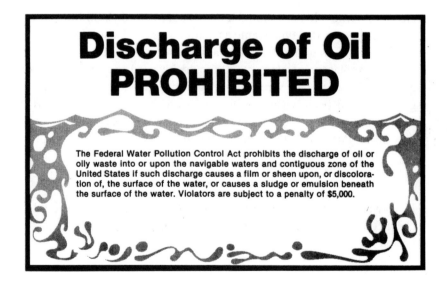

Discharge of Oil PROHIBITED

The Federal Water Pollution Control Act prohibits the discharge of oil or oily waste into or upon the navigable waters and contiguous zone of the United States if such discharge causes a film or sheen upon, or discoloration of, the surface of the water, or causes a sludge or emulsion beneath the surface of the water. Violators are subject to a penalty of $5,000.

Fig. 4-5. Water pollution placard. No person may operate a vessel, except a foreign vessel or a vessel less than 26 feet in length, unless it has a placard at least 5 by 8 inches, made of durable material, fixed in a conspicuous place in the machinery spaces, or at the bilge and ballast pump control station, stating the above.

Important! After the oil has been drained and the filter changed (see below), precautions for cleanliness must be taken before the new oil is added (most bearing failures are caused by dirt). Any funnel, hose, or container used to transfer the oil must be thoroughly cleaned, as must the top surfaces of the oil cans. The area around the oil fill cap (usually on the rocker arm cover) must also be free of foreign matter. Only then is the new oil to be added.

The manufacturer's manual specifies the amount of oil required. Do not mix brands of lubricating oil. After the new oil has been added, the engine should be operated for a few minutes and a check made for oil leaks. The engine should then be stopped for about five minutes (to allow the oil to drain into the sump) and the dipstick checked for proper oil level; if it's below the FULL mark, oil should be added. It is important not to overfill—this will tend to allow the oil to be churned (by the rotating crankshaft) and may cause overheating of the engine.

Spare lubricating oil should be carried on board.

Filter Change

A new filter element should be installed whenever the oil is changed; cleaning a filter element should not be attempted. Most oil filters are of the spin-on cartridge type (same as automotive) and a special clamp-on type wrench is required for removal (Fig. 4-6). If a gasket is included with the replacement element, it should be used in place of the old gasket. *Caution:* Make sure that both gaskets are not installed. The new gasket should be lubricated with oil before installation and the filter tightened *hand tight;* excessive tightening is not necessary. After the new oil is added, the engine should be operated to check for leaks.

Oil Cooler

If seawater is circulated through the oil cooler, the zincs should be checked every two months and replaced if necessary (see "Zincs" in Chapter 3).

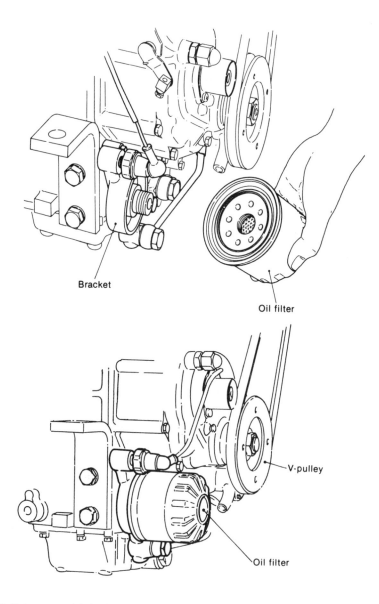

Fig. 4-6. Spin-on type lubricating oil filter (Courtesy Yanmar Diesel Engine (USA), Inc.)

CHAPTER 5

The Combustion Air System

THE combustion of diesel fuel (or any fossil fuel) requires oxygen and the oxygen is obtained from the air. But only about 21 percent of the air is oxygen (the rest is mostly nitrogen); thus, a large volume of air is needed to provide the oxygen required. To burn one gallon of diesel fuel a theoretical minimum of 1,500 cubic feet of air is required, but to insure efficient combustion most engines require about 3,000 cubic feet. Thus, an engine that consumes one gallon of fuel per hour requires one large ($20' \times 20' \times 7^1/2'$), roomful of air every hour. To reduce the noise created by the inrushing air, some larger engines are equipped with air silencers.

Cleanliness of the air is of prime importance! Even a minute quantity of dust, sand, or soil can cause severe damage to the engine. Most foreign matter will act as an abrasive that will score valves, piston rings, and cylinder walls; this will result in valve leakage and piston blow-by (leakage between the piston and cylinder wall). From the cylinder walls the foreign matter will be picked up by the lubricating oil and (unless completely removed by the lubricating oil filter) circulated to the bearings. This results in excessive wear of the bearing material and possible scoring of the bearing journal (the hardened steel shaft).

To prevent the entry of foreign matter with the combustion air, all engines should be fitted with an air cleaner. Some argue that an air cleaner is not necessary in coastal waters because sea air is always pure. Not so! An offshore breeze can include sand, dust, smoke, or smog. In a marina or anchorage, an earthmoving construction project upwind of your boat will guarantee that the combustion air is saturated with abrasive soil.

Marine diesel engines are equipped with a variety of air cleaners. An automotive type cleaner with a replaceable paper element is used on some small engines. Filters with a washable polyurethane element (Fig. 5-1) are also used. Oil bath cleaners (Fig. 5-2) are used on larger engines; the air is first directed downward and then upward and the momentum of the heavier dirt particles allows them to be captured by the

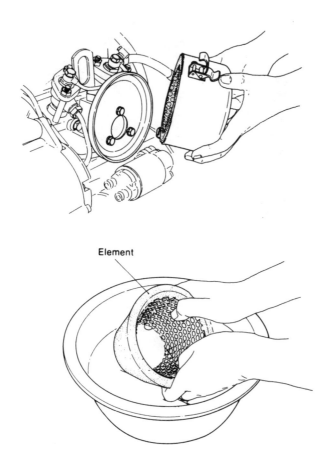

Element

Fig. 5-1. Air cleaner with washable element (Courtesy Yanmar Diesel Engine (USA), Inc.)

oil. Dry elements that can be cleaned with compressed air are also used. Some air cleaners are built into the air silencer.

THE COMBUSTION AIR PATH

From the atmosphere, air enters the engine compartment through openings that must be large enough to handle the required volume of air and arranged so that any water entering with the air is separated from the air (water is detrimental to a paper element). From the engine room, the combustion air passes through the silencer (if fitted), air cleaner, and, on

Fig. 5-2. Oil bath air cleaner for marine engines (Courtesy Detroit Diesel Corp.)

conventional four-stroke-cycle engines, into the inlet manifold where it is distributed to each intake valve. At the start of the inlet stroke the camshaft opens the inlet valve and the air flows into the cylinder during the downward movement of the piston. At the start of the compression stroke, the camshaft allows the valve spring to close the inlet valve and at the end of the compression stroke the combustion air (now hot and at a high pressure) is ready for fuel injection.

On a two-stroke-cycle engine, combustion air from the air cleaner enters the scavenging air blower and is discharged into the air box. As the piston approaches its downward position, the exhaust valves open and allow some of the spent combustion products to escape. Further movement of the piston uncovers the air inlet port, allowing scavenging air to blow out the remaining combustion products through the still-open exhaust valves, and charge the cylinder with clean combustion air. As the piston starts its upward movement, the exhaust valves close and the piston closes off its air inlet port to start compression of the combustion air. After the piston completes its upward movement, the hot, compressed air is ready for fuel injection.

To optimize the performance of an actual engine, intake and exhaust valves do not open and close at the exact top and bottom dead center. Also, fuel injection occurs before top dead center. The theoretical and actual opening and closing of the valves is shown in Figures 5-3 and 5-4.

NATURAL ASPIRATION AND SUPERCHARGING

A naturally aspirated engine is a conventional four-stroke-cycle engine in which the combustion air is sucked in (aspirated) by the downward movement of the piston during the intake stroke. Actually, the downward movement of the piston creates a partial vacuum in the cylinder and the more highly pressurized atmospheric air flows into the vacuum zone above the piston. In the design of the engine every effort is made to minimize obstruction to the inflow of combustion air: an air cleaner with a large element area is used, sharp corners are eliminated from the intake manifold, and inlet valves are made as large as feasible. Yet, the air pressure in the cylinder at the end of the intake stroke is always less than atmospheric pressure. This is undesirable because when the pressure of the air is reduced, it becomes lighter and there are fewer pounds of air available for the combustion of fuel.

Supercharging is the process of increasing an engine's horsepower by use of a fan, blower, or air compressor to increase the pressure of the air during the inlet stroke. The increased air pressure provides more pounds of air and more fuel can be combusted. The engine must, of course, be designed to withstand the greater pressures and temperatures associated with increased horsepower. On today's diesel engines, supercharging is accomplished by the use of a turbocharger, a gas turbine connected to a rotary air compressor and powered by the engine's exhaust (Figs. 5-5 and 5-6).

The turbine-driven air compressor raises the pressure of the air; but, whenever the pressure of air is raised, its temperature is automatically increased. Hot air has less density (less pounds per cubic foot) than cool air; therefore, most turbocharged diesel engines are equipped with air coolers that reduce the air temperature to permit charging the cylinder with high-pressure, low-temperature air. This provides the engine with the maximum feasible pounds of air (for a given size cylinder) and permits the injection of the maximum amount of fuel.

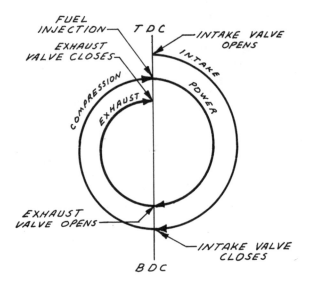

Fig. 5-3. Theoretical valve timing—four-stroke cycle

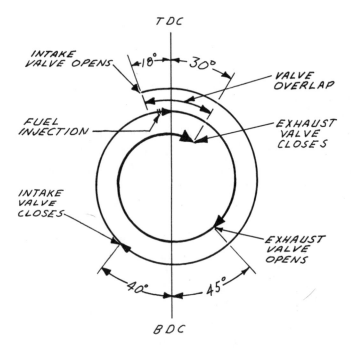

Fig. 5-4. Actual valve timing—four-stroke cycle

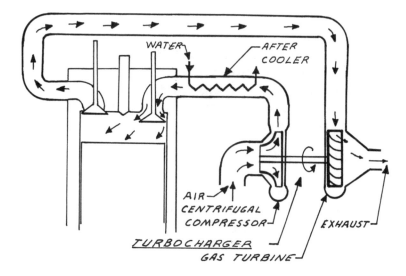

Fig. 5-5. Turbocharger with aftercooler

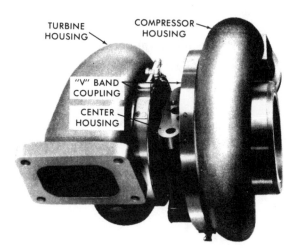

Fig. 5-6. Typical turbocharger (Courtesy Detroit Diesel Corp.)

In the air cooler, heat from the air is transferred to the water (raw or fresh) circulated through the tubes of the cooler. Because the combustion air flows through the air cooler after it has been discharged from the compressor, the cooler is known as an "aftercooler."

On two-stroke-cycle engines, the scavenging air blower provides a supercharging effect. Shortly after the piston starts its upward movement, the exhaust valves close while the air inlet port is still uncovered (Fig. 5-7). This allows the air in the cylinder to attain the same pressure as the air box pressure. Two-cycle engines can also be fitted with a turbocharger and air cooler when more effective supercharging is desired. The air cooler is located between the turbocharger and the scavenging air pump and in this position it is referred to as an "intercooler."

A turbocharger is not effective at low engine speeds; a high rate of flow of exhaust gases is required for the turbine to attain its effective speed of about 20,000 to 40,000 RPM. At high throttle settings, the turbocharger can increase the horsepower of an engine by 40–50 percent, as compared to a naturally aspirated engine of the same size.

THE RUNAWAY DIESEL

Danger! A diesel engine will continue running as long as it is supplied with air and fuel, and there is sufficient compression to provide the ignition temperature. If one of the three ingredients is removed, the engine will stop. The fuel ingredient consists of the diesel oil supplied by the fuel injection system but can also include lubricating oil that may leak into and combine with the combustion air. If a substantial amount

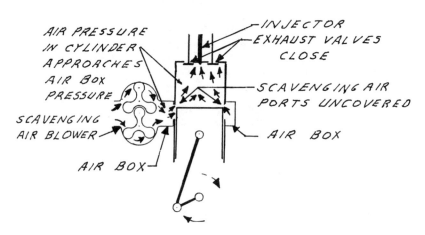

Fig. 5-7. Supercharging effect of the scavenging air blower

of lubricating oil is introduced, it may cause the engine to overspeed because the engine governor only controls the injection of diesel oil. This is a runaway condition and is dangerous because the engine may fly apart, as it is not designed to withstand the stress associated with the excessive speed. Therefore, shutting off the supply of combustion air is the only sure method of stopping a diesel engine.

Failure of an oil seal in a scavenging air pump or in the air compressor of a turbocharger will allow lubricating oil to unite with the combustion air. Oil leaks of this type are more prevalent on two-cycle engines and some engines are equipped with a manually operated air inlet baffle to insure that the engine can be stopped.

Although the probability of a runaway condition is extremely remote, every engine operator should thoroughly understand that *the only positive method of stopping a diesel engine is to shut off its supply of combustion air*. If an air inlet baffle is not provided, a pillow, jacket, or any object can be used to seal off the air inlet.

COMBUSTION AIR SYSTEM MAINTENANCE

Air Silencer

The air silencer requires no service, but a periodic inspection should be made to insure that the internal screens, perforated metal parts, or other parts are not corroded. Corroded parts may permit metal particles to contaminate the combustion air.

Air Cleaner

The frequency of air cleaner inspection is best established by experience, but the manufacturer's manual may specify the service interval. A partially clogged filter will result in loss of power and excessive fuel consumption. On a turbocharged engine, a partially clogged filter may damage the oil seals, resulting in oil leakage into the combustion air. A fully clogged filter will stop the engine.

The manufacturer's manual will provide instructions for the cleaning or replacement of the element. The oil in oil bath filters should be replaced at intervals specified by the manufacturer or when the oil appears to be laden with foreign matter. Automotive type paper filter elements should be replaced rather than an attempt made at cleaning.

Turbocharger

Some turbochargers are fitted with their own lubricating oil filter; the filter element should be replaced at intervals specified by the manufacturer. After installation of a new filter element, it may be necessary to prime the oil system (manually fill the oil passages with oil) before starting the engine to insure that oil is immediately supplied to the bearings. The manufacturer's manual will specify if priming is required and will describe the procedure.

Intercooler and Aftercooler

If seawater is circulated through a cooler, inspect pencil zincs every two months; replace if necessary (see Chapter 3).

Air Box Drain

On two-cycle engines the air box moisture drain should be checked frequently to insure that it is unclogged (Fig. 5-8).

AIR BOX
DRAIN TUBE

Fig. 5-8. Air box drain—two-cycle engine (Courtesy Detroit Diesel Corp.)

CHAPTER 6

The Fuel System

THE fuel system is required to deliver to the engine a precise amount of fuel at the precise time in a precisely defined spray pattern. To form the spray pattern, a minute amount of fuel (millionths of a gallon) must be subjected to an extremely high pressure (1,500–6,000 psi) and must be delivered at very short intervals (hundredths of a second).

Diesel oil, as received at the fuel dock, contains dirt particles in suspension and may contain various microorganisms and water. Additional water may be introduced from the natural condensation of the moisture in the air in the fuel tank (when air is humid and nights are cool). These impurities must be filtered out of the fuel before it is delivered to the fuel injection pump. Even extremely small particles of foreign matter in the fuel will cause excessive wear and may clog the fuel pump or injectors. Water will rust the high-precision parts and will flash into steam in the tip of the injector, causing erosion of the tip. The water will ultimately unite with the sulfur in the fuel to form sulfuric acid. Also, water in the fuel provides the necessary medium in which fuel-eating microbes multiply (and clog filter elements and fuel piping). Diesel fuel contamination is a major problem that causes about 50 percent of all diesel engine breakdowns and results in expensive repairs.

The diesel engine fuel system (Fig. 6-1) actually consists of (1) a low-pressure fuel storage, filtration, and transfer system; and (2) the high-pressure fuel injection system.

LOW-PRESSURE SYSTEM

This system consists of the fuel tank(s), primary filter, fuel lift pump, secondary filter, the connecting piping, and the fuel return piping (from the injectors back to the fuel tank(s)).

Fuel tanks are made of steel, aluminum, and fiberglass. Galvanized steel tanks should not be used for diesel oil; the zinc from the coating will react with the sulfur present in all No. 2 diesel fuel to form a

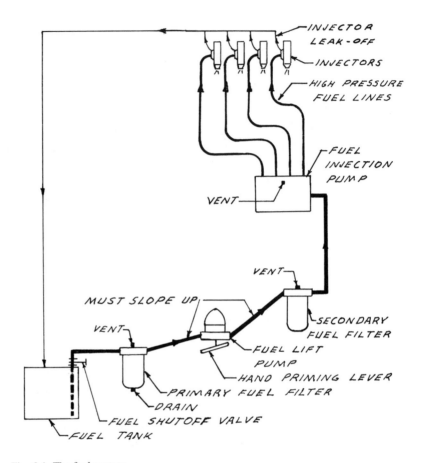

Fig. 6-1. The fuel system

precipitate that is detrimental to the fuel injection pump and the injectors. A proper fuel tank installation is shown in Fig. 6-2, although not all tanks are equipped with access plates (for cleanout) and a settlement sump with pump-out piping.

The primary filter should be of the moisture-absorbing type (Fig. 6-3), and preferably have a transparent bowl so that the trapped water will be visible and can be drained. In this type filter, water separation is attained by rapid changes in direction of the flow path; the heavier water particles and some impurities are thrown outward and collect in the bowl. Some of these filters can be equipped with an electric sensor that actuates an alarm when sufficient water has collected in the bowl to

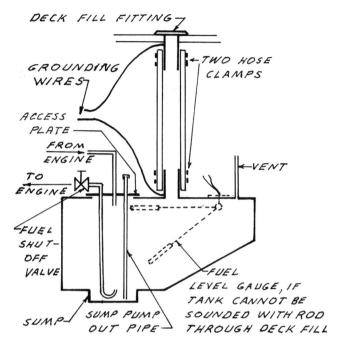

Fig. 6-2. The diesel fuel tank

warrant drainage. After water separation, the fuel flows through a replaceable paper element for removal of solid particles.

The fuel lift (or transfer) pump is usually of the automotive diaphragm type (Fig. 6-4). Most pumps are equipped with an external lever that permits operation of the pump when the engine is not running. The pump is normally located between the primary and secondary fuel filters to insure that water in the fuel is removed before it gets to the pump—the pumping action tends to form small water droplets that are difficult to separate from the fuel. On some engines, the fuel lift pump may be built into the fuel injection pump; electrically operated pumps are also used.

The secondary fuel filter (usually supplied as part of the engine) has a much finer replaceable element that filters out smaller particles than the primary filter. Secondary filters can be of the replaceable element type (Fig. 6-5) or of the spin-on type (similar to the lubricating oil filter of Fig. 4-6). Some secondary filters will also remove water but water separation should take place in the primary filter before it comes

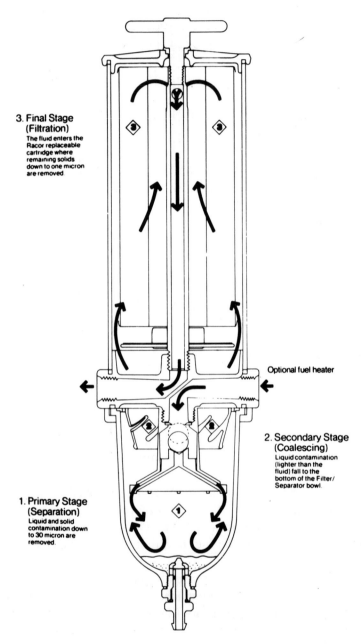

3. Final Stage (Filtration)
The fluid enters the Racor replaceable cartridge where remaining solids down to one micron are removed.

Optional fuel heater

2. Secondary Stage (Coalescing)
Liquid contamination (lighter than the fluid) fall to the bottom of the Filter/Separator bowl.

1. Primary Stage (Separation)
Liquid and solid contamination down to 30 micron are removed.

Fig. 6-3. Three-stage primary filter/water separator (Courtesy Racor Division, Parker Hannifin Corp.)

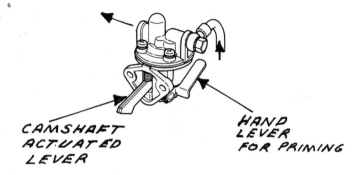

CAMSHAFT
ACTUATED
LEVER

HAND
LEVER
FOR PRIMING

Fig. 6-4. Diaphragm type fuel lift pump (Courtesy Yanmar Diesel Engine (USA), Inc.)

in contact with the replaceable filter elements. Water has a detrimental effect on paper filter elements.

HIGH-PRESSURE SYSTEM

This system consists of the fuel injection pump, the individual injectors, and the interconnecting high-pressure piping. The governor, which controls the amount of fuel delivered by the fuel injection pump, and the combustion chambers can be considered as adjuncts to the high-pressure system.

The early diesel engines were air injection engines; compressed air was mixed with a measured amount of fuel and injected into the cylinder with the fuel. The compressed air provided the energy for injection and atomized the fuel. The main disadvantage of this system was that a multistage compressor was required to provide the very high pressure air required for injection. The first mechanical, or solid, injection system was developed in 1910 and presently two systems are mostly used on small diesel engines: the in-line pump and the rotary distributor pump (Fig. 6-6).

The In-Line Pump

This system is also known as the jerk pump, Bosch pump, or individual pump. A separate pump is used for each cylinder. On very large engines the pump is located adjacent to its cylinder to keep the high-pressure fuel lines the same length. On smaller engines the pumps are built into a single housing that includes a camshaft (to actuate the pumps) and a lubricating oil sump.

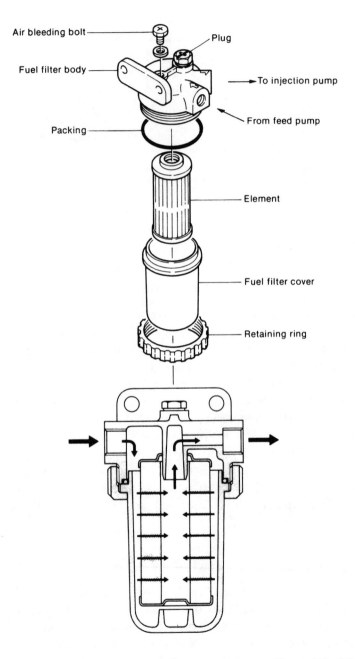

Fig. 6-5. Replaceable element type secondary fuel filter (Courtesy Yanmar Diesel Engine (USA), Inc.)

IN-LINE

ROTARY DISTRIBUTOR

Fig. 6-6. Rotary distributor and in-line fuel injection pumps (Courtesy Diesel Systems Division, Stanadyne Automotive Corp.)

Each pump consists of a reciprocating plunger that fits into a barrel. The plungers and barrels are individually lapped to attain the absolute minimum of radial clearance. Although these pumps have a constant stroke, they provide a variable delivery by means of a vertical slot, a helical slot, and rotation of the plunger relative to two ports in the barrel. Figure 6-7 demonstrates how variable delivery is accomplished.

In Figure 6-7A the plunger is rotated so that the vertical slot lines up with the spill port. When the plunger is in its lower position, fuel enters through the inlet port and fills the space above the plunger. As the plunger moves upward, the fuel is forced downward through the vertical slot and flows out through the spill port. No fuel is delivered by the pump; the effective stroke is zero.

In Figure 6-7B the plunger is rotated away from the spill port. Fuel enters through the inlet port and fills the space above the plunger. When the plunger moves up to where the top of the plunger closes off both ports, the fuel is compressed to a high pressure and delivered to the injector by means of the high-pressure fuel line. When the plunger moves up to where the helical groove lines up with the spill port, the fuel flows down the vertical slot, through the helical slot, and out through the

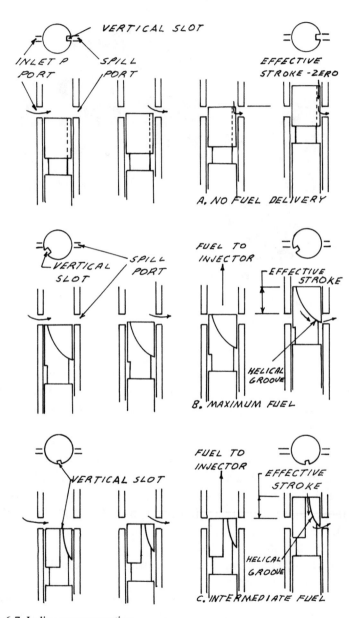

Fig. 6-7. In-line pump operation

spill port. This is the end of the effective stroke; in this position of the plunger, the pump delivers the maximum amount of fuel.

In Figure 6-7C the plunger is rotated to an intermediate position and the helical slot lines up with the spill port sooner. This reduces the effective stroke and the amount of fuel delivered.

The amount of fuel injected can be regulated by rotating the plunger to any position between no delivery and maximum delivery. Rotation of the plungers is attained by a gear attached to each plunger and rotated by a rack that engages all of the gears. Horizontal movement of the rack rotates all of the gears and varies the fuel delivery of all the pumps.

Unit Injector

This system is actually a simplification of the in-line pump system; the pump is built into the injector and the high-pressure fuel line is eliminated (Fig. 6-8). The unit injector is mounted on the cylinder head and the plunger is forced downward by a rocker arm, actuated by a

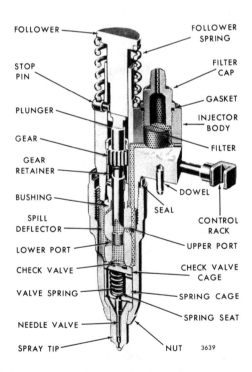

Fig. 6-8. The unit injector (Courtesy Detroit Diesel Corp.)

camshaft, to deliver fuel to the cylinder. Each unit injector has its own control rack attached to a control tube that is positioned by the governor.

Rotary Distributor Pump

In this system one injection pump with two opposed plungers is used to deliver fuel under pressure to all cylinders. Fuel is delivered into the space between the plungers by a rotary vane transfer pump; as the plungers move together, the fuel is subjected to a high pressure and flows into a rotary distributor (similar in principle to an automotive ignition distributor). The distributor's rotating fuel passage lines up with individual stationary passages that lead to each injector (Fig. 6-9). A metering valve at the inlet port regulates the amount of fuel entering the injection pump.

Rotary distributor pumps are more compact than the in-line pump system. Also, the distributor pump is lubricated by the diesel oil. The timing of the fuel delivery to each cylinder is established by the position of the drilled passageways in the distributor and, as the same pump is used for all cylinders, each injector receives the same amount of fuel. This results in a smooth-running engine, even at idling speed.

Governor

Unlike the automotive engine, where the throttle directly controls the flow of fuel, most diesel engines are equipped with a governor that keeps the engine operating at the speed called for by the governor setting. The manually operated throttle changes the governor setting. The governor prevents the engine from overspeeding when the load is momentarily reduced (e.g., by a following sea that lifts the boat's screw out of the water).

Most governors are of the centrifugal flyball weight type and are usually built into the fuel injector pump housing (Fig. 6-10). The spindle of the governor is driven by the engine and contains two weights that move outward as the speed is increased. This movement is opposed by a spring; the tension of the spring is controlled by the throttle. Movement of the flyball weights changes the position of a fuel control rod that is connected to the fuel control (rack or metering valve) of the fuel injection pump.

When the engine starts to speed up (due to a reduction in load) the flyball weights move outward, causing the fuel control rod to move in

Components:
1. Drive Shaft
2. Distributor Rotor
3. Transfer Pump Blades
4. Pumping Plungers
5. Internal Cam Ring
6. Hydraulic Head
7. Pressure Regulator Assembly
8. Governor
9. Automatic Advance
10. Housing
11. Metering Valve

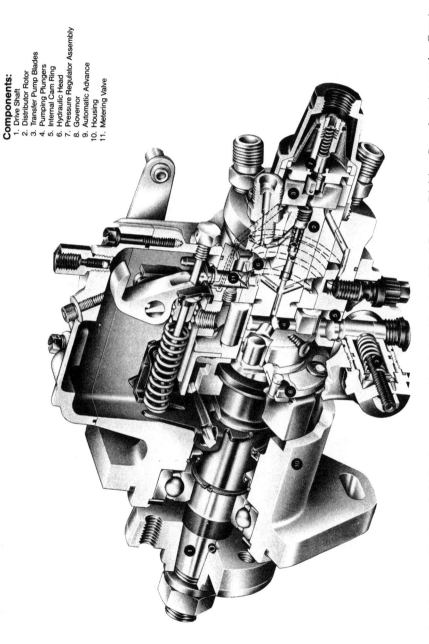

Fig. 6-9. Rotary distributor fuel injection pump—sectional view (Courtesy Diesel Systems Division, Stanadyne Automotive Corp.)

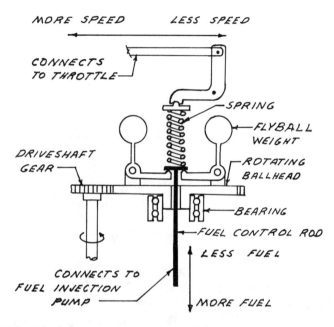

Fig. 6-10. The flyball governor

the "less fuel" direction. When the throttle is positioned for more speed, the spring is compressed, forcing the flyball weights inward; this moves the fuel control rod in the "more fuel" direction.

Vacuum, or diaphragm, governors are used on some engines and consist primarily of a butterfly valve and a diaphragm. To reduce engine speed, the throttle partially closes the butterfly valve, increasing the vacuum in the inlet manifold. This reduced pressure is transmitted by means of a tube to one side of a diaphragm, causing the diaphragm to deflect towards the negative pressure. The opposite side of the diaphragm is connected to the fuel injection pump speed control to move it into the direction of "less fuel." For increased speed, the butterfly valve is opened, reducing the vacuum and allowing the diaphragm to approach its undeflected position. This moves the speed control in the "more fuel" direction.

Solenoid
Some engines are equipped with a solenoid that must be energized to allow the governor to control engine speed. When the solenoid is not

energized, a spring moves the fuel injection pump speed control into the "no fuel" position. Usually the solenoid is wired into the ON position of the starter switch key.

Injectors

The fuel injector is also known as an atomizer, spray nozzle, spray valve, or fuel delivery valve, and is required to (1) deliver the fuel into the combustion chamber in a fine, foglike spray and (2) prevent compression and combustion pressure from entering the fuel supply line.

The injector consists primarily of a body, a spring-loaded valve, and a nozzle (Fig. 6-11). The body mounts on the cylinder head and includes the fuel supply and return fittings. The spring keeps the valve in the closed position until the injection pump delivers the high-pressure fuel. At that time the upward force of the high-pressure fuel, acting on

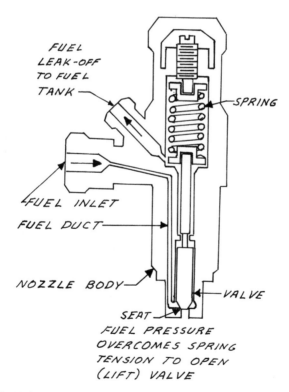

Fig. 6-11. Typical injector

the valve face, exceeds the downward force of the spring and the valve opens, allowing fuel to flow through the nozzle into the combustion chamber. The tip of the nozzle divides the liquid fuel into a fine spray for easy vaporization and combustion. When the fuel pressure is reduced, the spring snaps the valve back against its seat.

There are three basic nozzle tip configurations: the open, the pintle, and the multihole (Fig. 6-12). The open is the simplest and consists of a single orifice, but this arrangement provides the minimum amount of atomization. The pintle is an extension that protrudes through the orifice and provides an improved hollow cone-shaped spray. Both the open and the pintle are self-cleaning. The multihole discharges the fuel through two or more small holes and provides a very fine spray pattern. However, the multihole tip requires a higher fuel injection pressure and its small holes are subject to clogging.

A small amount of diesel fuel flows upward through the injector to cool and lubricate the moving parts and is then returned to the fuel tank by way of the injector leak-off piping.

Combustion Chambers

Since the fuel is delivered to the combustion chamber over a period of time (not instantaneously), efficient combustion depends on the thorough mixing of the oxygen in the air with the fuel during this interval. This mixing can be enhanced if a turbulent motion is imparted to the air while the fuel is sprayed into the combustion chamber. Various shapes of combustion chambers are utilized to attain turbulence and

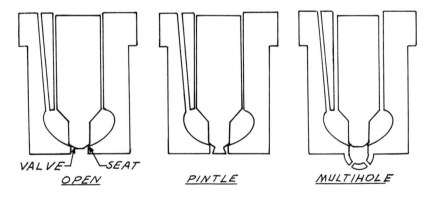

VALVE—— ——SEAT
OPEN   PINTLE   MULTIHOLE

Fig. 6-12. Injector tips

optimize the combustion process. The most common combustion chamber shapes are the following (Fig. 6-13).

1. The open or direct combustion chamber is the simplest; the top surface of the piston or the cylinder head is contoured to conform to the spray pattern.
2. The precombustion chamber is a small chamber in the cylinder head in which the fuel is preconditioned for combustion, most of which takes place in the main combustion chamber.
3. The turbulence chamber is spherical in shape and is located to the side of the main chamber. Combustion takes place primarily in the turbulence chamber; the burning fuel and air expand rapidly into the main chamber.
4. In the energy cell combustion chamber, fuel is sprayed across the top of the piston into an opposite chamber called an energy cell. Combustion is initiated primarily in the energy cell and then spreads into the main chamber.

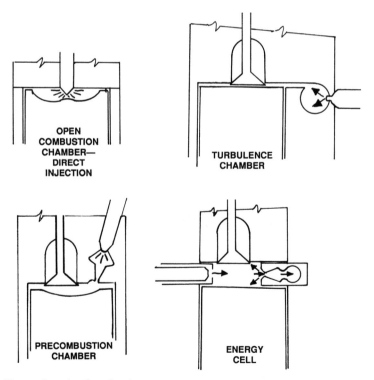

OPEN COMBUSTION CHAMBER— DIRECT INJECTION

TURBULENCE CHAMBER

PRECOMBUSTION CHAMBER

ENERGY CELL

Fig. 6-13. Types of combustion chambers

BLEEDING THE FUEL SYSTEM

Air in the fuel may cause an engine to misfire or knock but usually this situation will bring an engine to a complete stop. Except for some distributor type fuel injection pumps that include a self-purging feature, most fuel injection pumps cannot tolerate air in the fuel. The air must be removed from the fuel before the engine can be restarted.

Air entry into the fuel system may be caused by any one of the following conditions.

1. Running out of fuel.
2. A low fuel level (the fuel inlet pipe may become uncovered when the vessel heels or rolls).
3. Operating the engine with the fuel shutoff valve closed.
4. Draining a fuel filter (unless the fuel level in the tank is above the level of the filter).
5. A leak in the fuel piping between the fuel tank and the suction side of the lift pump (unless the fuel level in the fuel tank is substantially above the level of the lift pump).

The fuel piping on the suction side of the lift pump is usually under a pressure less than atmospheric; the smallest hole in the piping will permit air to enter and accumulate in the fuel injection pump until it becomes airbound and stops pumping. A loose tubing fitting or a damaged thread may be the source of an air leak. Copper tubing exposed to continuous vibration may develop cracks that allow the entry of air.

Removal of the air is called "bleeding" or "purging" the fuel system. The air is first removed from the low-pressure system by manually operating the lift pump and opening the bleed fittings on the secondary filter and on the fuel pump. Then, if necessary, the air is bled from the high-pressure fuel lines by loosening the fittings at the injectors and cranking the engine with the starter. The procedure for most engines is as follows (Fig. 6-1).

1. Make sure there is fuel in the tank.
2. Make sure the fuel shutoff valve is open and the fuel pump solenoid, if fitted, is energized (starter switch key is in the ON position).
3. Loosen the bleed fitting(s) on top of the secondary fuel filter.

4. Operate the priming lever on the fuel lift pump until a flow of clear fuel (no bubbles) flows from the vent fitting(s). Then tighten the vent fittings.

    If the cam that operates the lift pump is in the maximum lift position, the priming lever will be inoperative. The engine must then be rotated with the starter until the priming lever can be operated.

    Some engines are equipped with a priming pump that is built into the fuel injection pump. Electric fuel pumps are also used.

5. Loosen the bleed fitting on the body of the fuel injection pump (or loosen the fuel inlet fitting if a bleed fitting is not provided) and operate the lift pump until clear fuel is flowing from the fitting. Then tighten the fitting.

The air has now been bled from the low-pressure system and an attempt should be made to start the engine. Usually it will start; if not, the high-pressure fuel lines must be bled, using the following procedure.

1. Set the throttle in the maximum speed position and energize the fuel solenoid.
2. Loosen the high-pressure fuel line nuts at the injectors.
3. Crank the engine with the starter until clear fuel is discharged from all the high-pressure fuel line fittings. Crank at 10-second intervals to prevent overheating of the starter motor.

If the engine is equipped with a decompression arrangement (which relieves the compression pressure in the cylinder), hold the lever in the decompression position during cranking to reduce the load on the battery.

After clear fuel is discharged from the high-pressure fuel line fittings, stop cranking and tighten the nuts.

The high-pressure system is now bled. Start the engine and let it operate for about 10 minutes. Check for fuel leaks, especially at the high-pressure fuel line nuts. Then stop the engine and wipe up all the fuel oil; it must not be allowed to collect in the bilges.

Detailed instructions for bleeding the fuel system are included in the manufacturer's manual. Every boat operator should practice bleeding the fuel system on his boat's engine until he is proficient. A bad load of fuel may necessitate the immediate replacement of a filter element; bleeding of the fuel system must follow.

The priming process may be time consuming if a large volume of air must be purged from the filters and fuel line by manual operation of the lift pump. The purging process can be expedited by filling the filter bowl with clean fuel, prior to reinstallation, or through a fitting at the top of the filter (less air to be removed). Separate pumps are sometimes used to facilitate priming. Figure 6-14 shows the installation of an electric priming (only) pump and check valve. Figure 6-15 shows a "hand-squeeze" primer bulb (usually used for outboard gasoline engine fuel systems) installed in the fuel line.

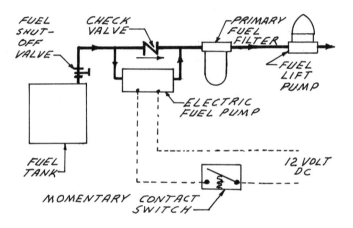

Fig. 6-14. Electric fuel priming pump

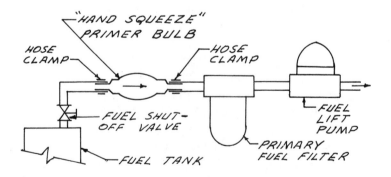

Fig. 6-15. Primer bulb for fuel system priming (Courtesy Capistrano Marine)

FUEL SYSTEM MAINTENANCE

In performing the following maintenance items, every effort must be made to prevent the entry of dirt and lint (from rags). Usually no other fuel system maintenance is required, but the manufacturer's manual should be studied for detailed instructions. To prevent the possibility of maladjustment and the entry of foreign matter, other fuel system components should not be disturbed if the engine is operating satisfactorily.

Fuel Tank

The presence of water in the fuel is always a possiblity. To destroy the algaelike organism that thrives and multiplies in the dark warm fuel-water atmosphere, the use of a biocide is recommended. The biocide should be added at every fueling; instructions are on the container. These microbes, if allowed to multiply, will completely clog the primary filter (stopping the engine) and even the fuel line.

Every few years the tank should be cleaned to remove the sediment that tends to collect at the bottom. Unless the tank is equipped with access covers (a float gauge mounting plate will provide limited access), the task is difficult and it will probably be necessary to rely on flushing. Tanks have been removed from boats to permit more thorough flushing and drainage through the fill connection. Commercial tank-cleaning contractors are available and should be consulted before removing a tank for cleaning.

Primary Fuel Filter

The filter bowl should be checked frequently (particularly after every fueling) and drained if water is present (Fig. 6-16). If the level of the fuel in the tank is lower than the filter, the top of the filter will have to be vented to permit drainage. *Caution:* If the fuel tank is below the primary fuel filter, the fuel shutoff valve must be closed before attempting to drain the filter. Otherwise, the water in the bottom of the filter may be sucked back into the fuel tank.

The replaceable filter element should be changed every 250 operating hours or at least once each season (unless more frequent changes are specified by the manufacturer). A spare filter element should be carried on board.

After draining or element replacement, the fuel system must be bled.

Fig. 6-16. Primary fuel filter with spin-on filter element, see-through bowl, and electrical probe to indicate presence of water (Courtesy Racor Division, Parker Hannifin Corp.)

Fuel Lift (Transfer) Pump

The diaphragm should be inspected and replaced if there is any evidence of pinhole leaks. Diaphragm leakage is usually indicated by dripping from the drain hole in the bottom of the pump.

Pumps attached to the fuel injection pump and electric pumps require no maintenance.

Secondary Fuel Filter

The element of this filter should be replaced (Fig. 6-17) every 250 operating hours or at least once each season (unless more frequent changes are specified by the manufacturer). After filter replacement, the fuel system must be bled.

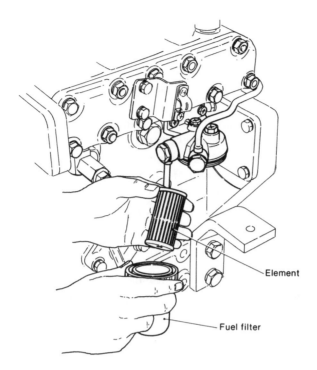

Fig. 6-17. Secondary fuel filter element replacement (Courtesy Yanmar Diesel Engine (USA), Inc.)

General Precautions

The cleanliness of the fuel and regular servicing of the filters cannot be overemphasized. Dirt is the archenemy of the fuel injection pump and injectors.

Caution: After fuel filter servicing, wipe up all fuel oil, especially from wiring; diesel oil has a detrimental effect on the insulation.

Danger! High-pressure diesel oil spray. Some mechanics advocate testing a fuel injector by removing it from the engine, attaching it to its high-pressure fuel line and cranking the engine to observe the spray pattern emitted from the tip of the injector. Injectors can be tested in this manner but this is a dangerous practice. The fuel sprayed from the tip of an injector is subjected to a very high pressure and attains a velocity that will enable it to penetrate the human skin if the spray is allowed to hit any part of the body. Penetration may be deep enough to reach the bloodstream and cause infection and even blood poisoning. A crack in a high-pressure fuel line or a defective high-pressure fitting may also emit a high-pressure spray. Keep hands, fingers, and arms well away from a high-pressure spray stream and arrange for repair at the first opportunity.

Danger! Fire. Do not bleed a fuel system while the engine is hot—diesel oil from the bleed fittings may contact a hot surface and ignite.

Most fires on diesel engine installations are caused by diesel oil from a leaking fitting or cracked fuel line contacting a hot surface. In case of fire, the engine must be immediately stopped and the fuel shutoff valve closed. If the fuel shutoff valve is not in an accessible location, a means of remote operation should be provided. It is sometimes advantageous to install an additional valve in a more accessible location.

Electric fuel pumps should be wired so that they are de-energized (stopped) when the engine is shut down to prevent feeding the fire after the engine is stopped.

The best precaution is the installation of an automatic Halon type fire extinguisher system in the engine compartment.

CHAPTER 7

The Exhaust System

THE exhaust system is required to (1) discharge the combustion products to the atmosphere, (2) suppress engine noise, and (3) prevent the entry of water into the engine. Water will tend to enter the engine by way of the exhaust manifold and then through the exhaust valves. Moisture will rust the exhaust valve stems and make them stick. In the cylinder, moisture will rust the cylinder walls and piston rings. If an attempt is made to start the engine when there is an appreciable amount of water in the cylinder, broken pistons and a cracked head are probable (water cannot be compressed). Also, the outer surface of the exhaust system must remain relatively cool while conducting hot exhaust gasses.

The path of exhaust flow starts in the cylinder after the power stroke when the combustion products are forced out by the piston (four-stroke cycle) or blown out by the scavenging air (two-stroke cycle). The hot gasses then pass through the exhaust valve(s) and into the exhaust manifold; the outer surface of the manifold is kept cool by means of a water jacket. From the manifold the combustion products are conveyed to the atmosphere by either the dry exhaust system or one of several water-cooled systems.

DRY EXHAUST

This system consists of a flexible metallic hose that connects the exhaust manifold outlet to a vertical exhaust pipe that extends several feet above the top of the cabin superstructure; an automotive type muffler may be inserted in the vertical exhaust pipe. A drain trap and drain valve are located at the bottom of the vertical exhaust pipe to capture rain and atmospheric condensation before it can drain into the exhaust manifold. The piping attains a high temperature and must be insulated and/or shielded (Fig. 7-1).

The advantage of this system is its simplicity, but noise suppression is minimal and the flexible hose, muffler, and exhaust pipe tend to

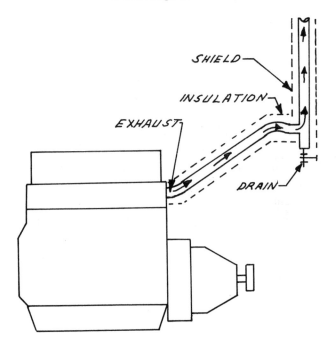

Fig. 7-1. Dry exhaust

rust out because of exposure to high temperatures. As no cooling water is required, it is the only exhaust system that can be used with a keel cooler system (no raw water). The dry exhaust system is commonly used on commercial fishing boats where engine noise is more acceptable than exhaust piping in a fish hold.

WATER-COOLED EXHAUST ON A POWERBOAT

On recreational powerboats, the engine's exhaust manifold is usually substantially above the waterline. A down-sloping elbow (mixer elbow), with a raw water inlet fitting, is attached to the outlet of the manifold. Raw water is supplied to the fitting and sprayed into the combustion products; this reduces the temperature and pressure of the exhaust gasses and consequently reduces engine noise. The cooled gasses and water are discharged to the atmosphere through a down-sloping pipe that extends through the transom. If additional noise reduction is required, a silencer can be installed in the run of exhaust pipe (Fig. 7-2).

If the exhaust manifold is too close to the waterline to provide the required downward slope of the exhaust pipe, an S-shaped manifold riser is used in place of the down-sloping elbow. Usually the riser is

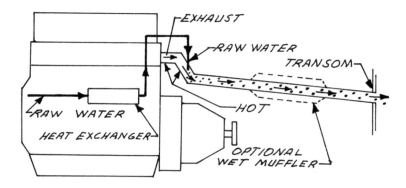

Fig. 7-2. Water-cooled exhaust—powerboat

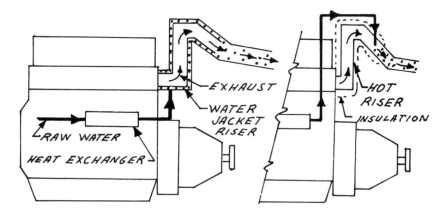

Fig. 7-3. Water-cooled exhaust with manifold riser—powerboat

water cooled and includes an arrangement for introducing the water into the exhaust gasses (Fig. 7-3).

The down-slope of the exhaust system is of prime importance to prevent the backflow of seawater from reaching the exhaust manifold. Backflow can occur when the engine is not running and a large wake from a passing powerboat strikes the transom. A following sea can also cause backflow when underway. A flapper at the exhaust outlet is commonly used to minimize backflow; also, a check valve in the exhaust pipe and a manually operated full-flow valve (kept closed when the engine is not running) have been used.

Danger! Any portion of the exhaust piping that is not cooled by a water jacket and is upstream of the raw water inlet is very hot and must be insulated.

WATER-COOLED EXHAUST ON A SAILBOAT

The exhaust system for sailboats is more complicated because the system must be designed to prevent the entry of seawater when the boat is under sail and the engine is not operating. This task is made more difficult because on sailboats the engine is located lower than on powerboats, placing the manifold closer to the waterline (especially when the boat is heeled to the side on which the manifold is located). On large sailboats, the manifold is actually below the waterline. Two systems are commonly in use, the standpipe muffler and the water lift muffler.

The Standpipe Muffler

The standpipe muffler (Fig. 7-4) is mounted above the waterline and on the centerline of the vessel. The combustion products are conveyed from the exhaust manifold to the muffler by means of a pipe that is fitted with a water jacket (a pipe within a pipe). Raw water from the engine is circulated through the jacket and then piped to the top of the muffler, where it flows over a baffle and into the exhaust gasses. The combustion products enter the bottom of the muffler into a vertical pipe that extends several inches into the muffler. This internal pipe prevents the backflow of seawater into the exhaust manifold. From the muffler, the gas-water mixture flows through a down-sloping exhaust hose, through the transom, and into the atmosphere.

Water-Lift Muffler

The water-lift muffler (Fig. 7-5) is a more recent development that eliminates the need for a water-jacketed pipe (difficult to fabricate). The water-lift muffler is located below the exhaust manifold and near the vessel's centerline. Raw water from the engine enters a down-sloping elbow and unites with the combustion products. The mixture continues to flow downward into the muffler. One end of the muffler outlet pipe is near the bottom of the muffler and the other end is connected to the exhaust hose that loops well above the waterline before sloping down through the transom. The pressure of the exhaust gas forces the water and combustion products up the outlet pipe, into the exhaust hose, and overboard (Fig. 7-5).

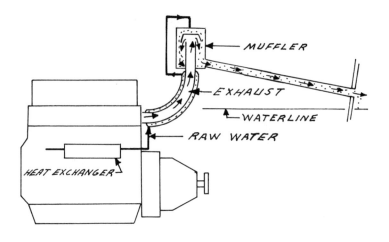

Fig. 7-4. Standpipe muffler—sailboat

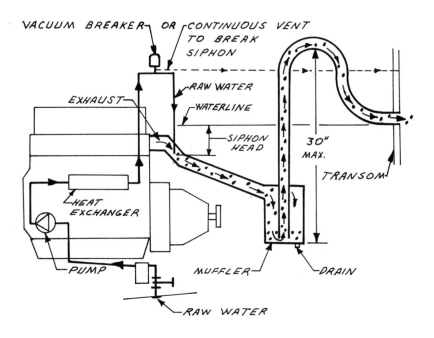

Fig. 7-5. Water-lift muffler—sailboat

However, the maximum lift that can be attained by a water-lift muffler is about 30 inches. If a greater vertical rise is desired, the muffler must be raised and a manifold riser installed. If the riser is not water cooled, it must be insulated.

The water-lift muffler provides excellent suppression of engine noise and is now used on most sailboats. But because the engine is usually installed so that the exhaust manifold is near or below the waterline, special precautions are required to prevent seawater from entering the exhaust manifold. There are three conditions to guard against: (1) backflow through the exhaust hose, (2) siphon through the raw water system, and (3) excessive cranking of the engine without starting.

Backflow

The exhaust hose between the muffler and the transom outlet must loop well above the waterline so that wave action, when the engine is not running, will not force water into the exhaust pipe (backflow) and fill the muffler, then the muffler inlet hose, and finally the exhaust manifold. The wave action may be caused by a following sea, the wake of a passing boat, or pitching at anchor. If a high loop is not possible, the exhaust hose should be fitted with a full-flow valve that must be open prior to starting the engine. As the valve must be opened and closed every time the engine is started and stopped, it must be in a readily accessible location.

Raw Water Siphon

When the engine is stopped, the raw water system is full of water from the sea cock to the exhaust system water inlet fitting. If the fitting is below the water level, a siphon condition is established and (if allowed to continue) the flow of raw water will fill the muffler and muffler inlet hose and then the manifold (Fig. 7-5). To prevent this occurrence, the water inlet hose must loop above the waterline and be equipped with a vacuum breaker valve. At the start of the siphon flow, the water in the upward loop is under a negative pressure. The vacuum breaker valve senses this negative pressure (vacuum) and opens, allowing air to enter and destroy the siphon condition.

Vacuum breaker valves, in a seawater application, tend to become clogged; a vent line is a more reliable alternative. However, the vent line discharges a stream of water whenever the engine is operating and it is often difficult to find a convenient location for the vent line outlet.

Excessive Cranking (Waterlogged Muffler)

As soon as the starter begins to crank the engine, the raw water pump starts discharging water into the water-lift muffler. But there is insufficient exhaust pressure to lift the water out of the muffler until the engine starts. If the engine fails to start after several cranking attempts, the muffler and inlet hose will fill with water. More cranking (if the battery still has sufficient charge) will force water into the manifold. Every water-lift muffler should be equipped with a drain valve or plug to permit draining the muffler after several unsuccessful attempts at starting.

EXHAUST SYSTEM MAINTENANCE

1. The vacuum breaker valve (if fitted) should be checked frequently to insure that the air inlet passage is not clogged (this can sometimes be accomplished by blowing into it). If clogged, it must be repaired or replaced.

    If a vent line is used in place of the vacuum breaker valve, the stream of discharged water should be frequently observed to insure that the vent line is not clogged.
2. If a separate fitting and hose are used to supply raw water for injection into the exhaust, the fitting and hose should be inspected once each season for foreign matter deposits that may restrict the flow of water. On raw water–cooled engines, the fitting and hose tend to become clogged with rust particles from the engine.
3. All exhaust system components, including gaskets, piping, hoses, and joints, should be frequently examined and defective components should be replaced. Hoses should be attached with two hose clamps at each end. Discoloration in the vicinity of a joint is usually an indication of an exhaust leak; it must be repaired immediately.

Danger! Carbon Monoxide. Carbon monoxide is a deadly poisonous gas and it is present in the exhaust of every diesel and gasoline engine. But the danger of carbon monoxide in recreational boating has only recently been recognized. The U.S. Coast Guard has recorded 24 deaths from 1984 to 1987; less serious carbon monoxide poisonings are mostly unreported because the symptoms are usually mistaken for flu or motion sickness. Infants, the elderly, and anyone with cardiovascular disease, anemia, lung disease, or high metabolism are especially affected. Extreme exposure can lead to unconsciousness and death; neuro-psychiatric problems may develop weeks later resulting in intellectual deterioration, memory impairment, and brain damage.

Unlike smoke, which consists of small solid particles suspended in air and moving only with the airstream, carbon monoxide is rapidly dispersed in air because it is a gas and rapidly diffuses in air, another gas. Diffusion is accelerated by an increase in temperature and occurs regardless of the pressure gradient, permitting carbon monoxide to, in effect, flow upstream in an air current. Diffusion permits carbon monoxide to rapidly disperse throughout an engine room and to penetrate the gap around a door or panel to contaminate an adjacent cabin. The hull and cabin superstructure of a boat usually create a tight envelope of small volume, so any source of carbon monoxide will create an immediate danger.

A leak in the engine exhaust system is the usual source of carbon monoxide. All exhaust system components (gaskets, piping, hoses, and particularly joints) should be frequently examined; discoloration is usually a sign of a leak. Rigid exhaust piping requires special attention because it receives vibrations from the engine that make it susceptible to

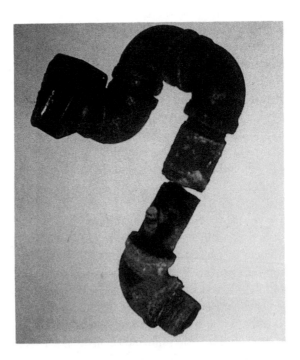

Fig. 7-6. A rigid exhaust pipe that failed due to prolonged vibration and corrosion

fatigue failure (Fig. 7-6). The danger exists on sailboats as well as on powerboats; in one case a crew member sleeping below was poisoned while the vessel was under sail and power (the cause was a defective exhaust hose).

As carbon monoxide gas is colorless, odorless, and nonirritating, its presence is imperceptible; fortunately, reliable and affordable detectors are available to warn of the presence of carbon monoxide before a dangerous concentration is attained. These sensors are "dose monitoring" and trigger an alarm only when the concentration of carbon monoxide persists for a sufficient length of time to create a hazardous condition (dose monitoring eliminates nuisance alarms). A dosimeter that changes color just before the concentration of carbon monoxide reaches a dangerous level is the least expensive sensor (Fig. 7-7). A 12-volt D.C.–powered alarm is also available; this device includes contacts that can sound a remote alarm, start a ventilating fan, or shut down an engine (Fig. 7-8).

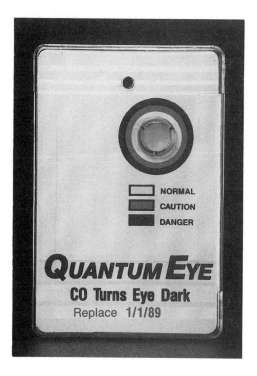

Fig. 7-7. Carbon monoxide dosimeter: 12-month life, actual size $1\frac{1}{2}'' \times 3''$ (Courtesy Quantum Group, Inc.)

Fig. 7-8. Carbon monoxide alarm: 12-volt D.C.–powered, actual size 4¼″ × 6¼″ (Courtesy Quantum Group, Inc.)

CHAPTER 8

The Starting System

MANY ingenious schemes have been used to start diesel engines.* But today's large marine engines are started by compressed air (admitted directly into the cylinders) and smaller engines by means of a 12-volt battery-powered starter motor (Fig. 8-1), the same as an automobile.

THE 12-VOLT STARTING SYSTEM

Presently two basic types of starters are used: the inertia and the preengaged starter. In the inertia starter, the pinion gear (the small gear that turns the flywheel) is keyed into a helical groove in the starter rotor shaft. When the starter is energized (and starts to rotate), the inertia of the pinion gear forces it to slide along the helical groove until it engages the ring gear of the flywheel. After engagement, the pinion gear rotates the ring gear until the engine starts. Then the higher speed of the ring gear drives the pinion back along the helical groove to its initial position.

The preengaged starter includes a large solenoid that operates a lever to first engage the pinion into the ring gear. After the pinion is fully engaged, the starter motor is energized to rotate the engine. The preengagement of the pinion provides a more positive gear contact and extends the life of the gears.

Starter motors require high current flow and large-diameter electric cables. To minimize cable length, a starter solenoid (actually a relay) is mounted on the starter and controlled by low-current wiring that extends to a key-operated switch at the control panel. When the key is placed in the START position, the starter solenoid is energized, providing current flow directly from the battery to the starter.

---

*The following systems that do not depend on a storage battery have been used to start marine diesel engines: gasoline or donkey engine, hydropneumatic starter, compressed air starter motor, inertia starter, shotgun starter, and the hand crank.

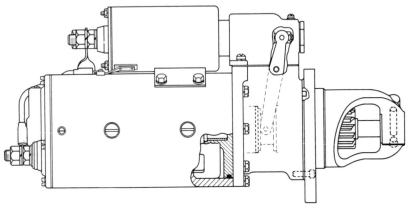

Fig. 8-1. Typical starting motor (Courtesy Caterpillar Inc.)

Caution: Do not crank the engine for more than 20 seconds at a time. The high current flow tends to overheat and damage the starter. Allow at least a one-minute cool-off period between each attempt to start.

The current for starting is supplied by a storage battery and the battery is recharged by an engine-driven alternator or generator, the same as in an automobile except that a heavier-duty battery is required (Fig. 8-2). Most boats are equipped with two batteries or banks of batteries, one for engine starting and the other for electrical auxiliaries (lights, radio, navigation equipment, etc.). The batteries are recharged by the alternator/generator when the engine is running. Other boats have a four-position switch (OFF, NO. 1, BOTH, and NO. 2). Batteries are best charged separately. The switch should be placed in the NO. 1 or NO. 2 position, but not in the BOTH position. Charging both batteries simultaneously (the switch in the BOTH position) takes longer and reduces battery life. In addition, if the charging system fails, the battery with the lower charge will drain the battery with the higher charge. This may result in neither battery having sufficient charge to start the engine.

Caution: Always reserve a charged battery for engine starting (or a tow to the nearest port may be required).

Caution: When the engine is running, do not put the battery switch into the OFF position. This will immediately destroy electronic components in the battery-charging systems.

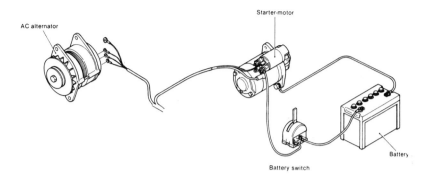

Fig. 8-2. Starter motor, alternator, and battery (Courtesy Yanmar Diesel Engine (USA), Inc.)

DECOMPRESSION

Some engines are equipped with a decompression lever. Normally this lever is left in the RUN position. In the RELEASE (or decompression) position, the lever mechanism holds the exhaust valves in the open position and the cranking load is substantially reduced as air is not compressed. Some small engines are equipped with a large flywheel and a decompression lever to permit starting by hand cranking. The lever is held in the RELEASE position and the engine is cranked by hand until a satisfactory speed is attained. The lever is then placed in the RUN position while still cranking. The momentum of the flywheel plus the cranking effort starts the engine.

Decompression may permit starting when the battery is low. The starter will attain a speed with decompression that may be great enough to start the engine when the lever is placed in RUN.

The decompression lever can also be used when bleeding the fuel system to minimize the drain on the battery.

In cold weather, cranking the engine in decompression before starting will break the grip of cold oil in the bearings and will provide oil to improve the seal about the piston. This will improve compression and aid starting.

Caution: Do not use the decompression lever to stop the engine, as serious damage to the exhaust valves and pushrods is probable.

STARTING AIDS

Any method employed to start the engine depends on attaining a cranking speed high enough to provide an ignition temperature. This is sometimes difficult to accomplish on a small engine because the heat
generated by compression tends to be absorbed by the relatively cool
metal mass of the engine. The surface-to-volume ratio of the combustion
space increases as engine size is reduced.

Presently there are two methods of providing heat to augment the
heat generated by the compression of the air: glow plugs and combustion
air preheat.

Glow Plugs

Glow plugs are threaded into the individual cylinders and are heated by
electric current from the battery. They attain a temperature of 1500°F
and most manufacturers specify that they be energized for about 15 to 30
seconds prior to starting.

Combustion Air Preheat

This method consists of an electric element or the ignition of a small
quantity of diesel oil in the inlet manifold to heat the combustion air. The
fuel is admitted by means of an electrically operated valve and is ignited
with a glow coil.

Excess Fuel

This arrangement to aid starting is used on some engines. It consists of
a lever on the fuel injection pump that is set, before starting, to deliver
an excess quantity of fuel when starting. After starting, the lever will
automatically disengage.

COLD WEATHER STARTING

Attempting to start an engine after it has been "cold soaked" at a low
temperature is always difficult because of the greater cooling effect of
the metal.

The most controversial cold-starting aid is ether. Some authorities
categorically state that it should never be used; others recommend its

use, but with caution. Ether vapor has a low ignition temperature and when sprayed into the combustion air inlet will aid starting. However, too much ether will cause damage to the engine. The problem occurs primarily when the ambient temperature drops below $-13°F$ $(-25°C)$ because ether tends to remain a liquid at these temperatures.*

Other (safer) cold-starting aids are as follows.

1. Use of decompression can aid cold starting. The lever is placed in the RUN position after the starter has attained a starting speed.
2. If an engine is to be frequently cold started, the installation of an extra battery will permit cranking for a longer overall period to aid starting.
3. As a last resort, the oil and coolant may have to be withdrawn from the engine, heated, and replaced to permit starting.

MAINTENANCE

Storage Battery

The electrolyte level should be checked frequently ($1/4$ to $1/2$ inch above the plates), particularly in hot weather. The battery should be checked periodically with a hydrometer and recharged if necessary. *Danger!* Do not allow an open flame near a battery that is being recharged; the gas generated is flammable.

Battery Cables

These should be checked for tightness at least once each season and greased to prevent corrosion.

---

*Methyl ether and dimethyl ether have a boiling point of $-25°C$ at atmospheric pressure.

CHAPTER 9

The Power Transmission System

THE power transmission system transfers the work generated by the engine to the propeller for propulsion of the vessel. Also, the system provides for ahead, neutral, and reverse operation of the propeller.

In most marine diesel engine installations, power from the engine is transmitted to the propeller by means of the inboard arrangement. On smaller vessels, the inboard/outboard arrangement is sometimes used, and diesel outboards (transom mounted) may be making a comeback. On some racing sailboats a hydraulic drive is used to permit locating the engine for optimum performance under sail.

THE INBOARD ARRANGEMENT

In this arrangement the engine is located at the approximate center or slightly aft of the center of the vessel. The transmission is usually attached to the after end of the engine to provide an in-line arrangement (Fig. 9-1). Use of a V-drive transmission permits reversing the engine to locate it further aft in the vessel (Fig. 9-2); this provides more accessible below-deck space forward of the engine.

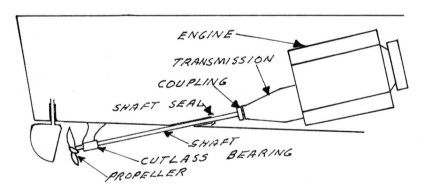

Fig. 9-1. The inboard in-line arrangement

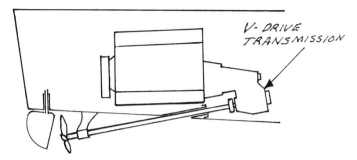

Fig. 9-2. The inboard V-drive arrangement

The Transmission

Power from the engine is transferred to the transmission and then to the shaft coupling. Attached to the after end of the coupling is a rotating shaft that pierces the hull; the propeller is attached to the after end of the shaft. Although not directly involved in the transmission of power, resilient mounts, a shaft seal, a cutlass bearing, and a transmission oil cooler (on larger engines) are also required. The engine is attached to the hull structure by means of the resilient mounts, which minimize the transmission of engine vibrations to the hull. The mounts also permit alignment of the engine-transmission assembly to the shaft. The shaft seal surrounds the shaft and prevents entry of water where the shaft pierces the hull. The cutlass (or strut) bearing, located just forward of the propeller, positions the after end of the shaft. On full-keel sailboats this shaft bearing is located in the after edge of the keel.

The transmission provides the ahead, neutral, and reverse features and may include a gear reduction in which the output shaft rotates at a lower speed than the input shaft. If a greater reduction is desired, a separate reduction gear unit (in its own housing) may be attached to the output shaft of the transmission. High-performance engines operate at high speeds but propulsion efficiency is best at low propeller speeds; gear ratios of 2:1 and 3:1 are common.

Three types of transmissions are in common use: (1) The manual planetary, (2) the hydraulic planetary, and (3) the two-shaft transmission.

Manual Planetary Transmission
The manual planetary transmission consists of the following major components (Fig. 9-3).

1. An outer gear with internal gear teeth.
2. A manually operated brake band that surrounds the outer gear.
3. A pinion and idler gear carrier, attached to the output shaft.
4. A manually operated clutch that locks the outer gear to the gear carrier.
5. A drive gear (the "sun" gear) attached to the input shaft. (In a planetary gear train, the center gear about which the other gears rotate or orbit is referred to as the sun gear.)
6. Idler gears that are attached to the carrier and mesh with the drive gear.
7. Pinion gears that are attached to the carrier and mesh with the idler gears and the outer gear.

For reverse operation the brake band is tightened by placing the lever in the REVERSE position; this prevents rotation of the outer gear. The drive gear rotates the idler gears and they in turn rotate the pinion gears. As the pinion gears are in mesh with the stationary outer gear, their rotation forces them to move relative to the internal gear (the pinion gears run inside of the outer gear) and, as the pinion gears are attached to the carrier, the movement of the pinion gears imparts a rotary motion to the carrier. The carrier rotation is in the opposite direction of drive gear rotation.

For neutral operation, the brake is released by the lever, allowing the outer gear to rotate. The pinion gears rotate but do not move; no motion is imparted to the carrier and the transmission output shaft does not rotate.

For ahead operation the brake remains released and the lever, when placed in the AHEAD position, engages a clutch that locks the carrier to the outer gear. All gears are locked together and the entire assembly rotates with the engine drive gear.

Hydraulic Planetary Transmission
The hydraulic planetary transmission is similar in operation to the manual planetary except that a self-contained oil pump is included and oil pressure is used to operate the brake band and clutch. Hydraulic shifting permits remote control from several stations (Figs. 9-4 and 9-5).

Two-Shaft Manual Transmission
The two-shaft manual transmission requires fewer parts than the planetary and usually no clutch adjustment. It is used on most newer small vessels (Fig. 9-6).

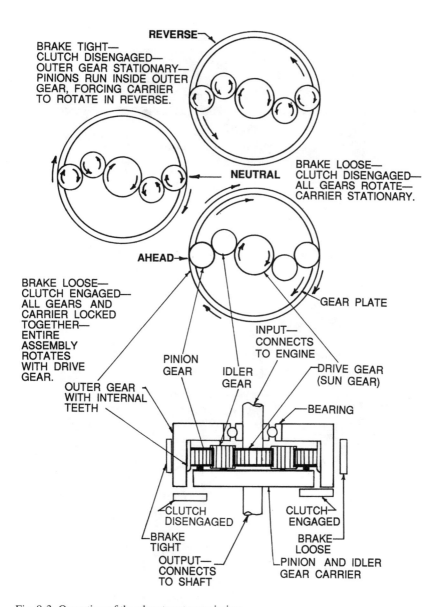

REVERSE

**BRAKE TIGHT—
CLUTCH DISENGAGED—
OUTER GEAR STATIONARY—
PINIONS RUN INSIDE OUTER
GEAR, FORCING CARRIER
TO ROTATE IN REVERSE.**

NEUTRAL

**BRAKE LOOSE—
CLUTCH DISENGAGED—
ALL GEARS ROTATE—
CARRIER STATIONARY.**

AHEAD

**BRAKE LOOSE—
CLUTCH ENGAGED—
ALL GEARS AND
CARRIER LOCKED
TOGETHER—
ENTIRE
ASSEMBLY
ROTATES
WITH DRIVE
GEAR.**

GEAR PLATE

INPUT—
CONNECTS
TO ENGINE

PINION
GEAR

IDLER
GEAR

DRIVE GEAR
(SUN GEAR)

OUTER GEAR
WITH INTERNAL
TEETH

BEARING

CLUTCH
DISENGAGED

CLUTCH
ENGAGED

BRAKE
TIGHT

BRAKE
LOOSE

OUTPUT—
CONNECTS
TO SHAFT

PINION AND IDLER
GEAR CARRIER

Fig. 9-3. Operation of the planetary transmission

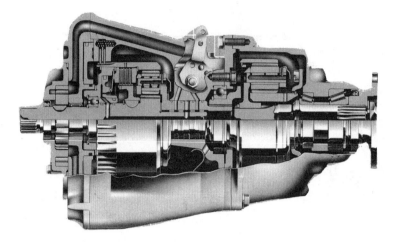

Fig. 9-4. In-line drive hydraulic transmission (Courtesy BorgWarner Marine and Industrial Transmissions)

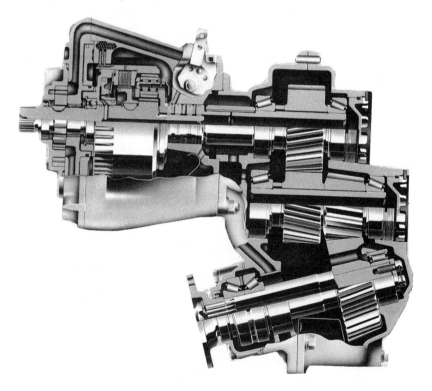

Fig. 9-5. V-drive hydraulic transmission (Courtesy BorgWarner Marine and Industrial Transmissions)

The major components consist of the following.

1. Two shafts (upper and lower).
2. A two-gear train for ahead propulsion.
3. A three-gear train for reverse; the second gear provides reverse rotation of the third gear.
4. A manually operated clutch located between the two gear trains and attached to the bottom shaft in a manner that permits it to slide on the shaft.

The first gear of each gear train is rigidly attached to the top shaft (rotated by the engine crankshaft). The last gear of each train fits about the lower shaft but is not attached to it. For ahead operation, the manual lever slides the clutch forward to engage the second gear of the ahead train; this, in effect, attaches the gear to the lower shaft and it is rotated in the ahead direction. When the clutch is slid aft to engage the third gear of the reverse train, the gear is in effect attached to the lower shaft and it is rotated in reverse. When the clutch is in its midposition (NEUTRAL), neither gear is engaged and there is no rotation of the lower (transmission output) shaft.

Caution: Engine speed should be at idle when shifting. On manual shift transmissions, the clutch lever must be pushed into the "home" position for ahead or reverse operation; a partially engaged clutch is detrimental to the transmission.

Freewheeling under Sail
Caution: When underway under sail, the propeller will tend to rotate (freewheel) the shaft. This may be detrimental to some transmissions; the manufacturer's manual should state if freewheeling is permissible. On some vessels the propeller may be locked by placing the transmission lever in the REVERSE position. If not, some other means of locking the shaft must be provided.

Transmission Oil
Usually an automotive automatic-transmission type oil (Dexron II) is used in marine transmissions. But some manufacturers specify an SAE 10W30, CC Class, for two-shaft manual transmissions. Different brands of oil should not be mixed.

On larger engines a transmission oil cooler is used to cool the oil; the construction of the oil cooler is similar to that of the heat exchangers shown in Figure 3-8.

The oil level in the transmission must be checked when the transmission is at its normal operating temperature, immediately after the engine is stopped; the oil drains back into the transmission from the oil cooler and oil lines after the engine is stopped.

For a cold level check it is first necessary to insure that oil is at the proper hot oil level, and the engine must be allowed to cool overnight. A mark can then be added to the dipstick at the level of the cold oil. This new mark can be used to check the oil level prior to starting the engine. Oil can be added to the new mark if necessary.

Danger! Do not remove the dipstick when the engine is running; hot oil may spray out of the dipstick opening and cause burns.

The oil must be changed at the intervals specified by the manufacturer or if there is any evidence of overheating (usually over 190°F); overheated oil gives off a smell that is different from new oil. In draining the oil it is important to insure that oil is removed from the cooler and cooler lines; this may require removal of the cooler lines from the transmission.

After draining the oil, it must be examined for metal particles and rubber particles. A few small metal particles are normal; however, large metal chips are an early sign of transmission failure. The transmission should be disassembled, inspected, and repaired by professionals. Rubber particles in the drained oil indicate cooler line wear. Each line should be inspected for cracks or fraying; the damaged lines should be replaced.

The amount of oil required to refill the transmission will depend on the size of the oil cooler and the size and length of the oil lines to and from the cooler. About three-fourths of the amount of oil removed should be added initially. The dipstick should then be installed and the engine should be run for about two minutes to fill the oil cooler and oil lines. Oil should then be added to the dipstick mark.

The Shaft Coupling

Alignment

The shaft coupling connects the transmission (or reduction gear) output shaft to the propeller shaft and also permits alignment of the engine transmission with the propeller shaft. The centerline of the propeller shaft must be concentric with the centerline of the transmission output shaft. The alignment process involves movement of the engine in horizontal, vertical, and angular directions by adjustment of the resilient engine mounts (Fig. 9-7). The base of each mount includes a slot to

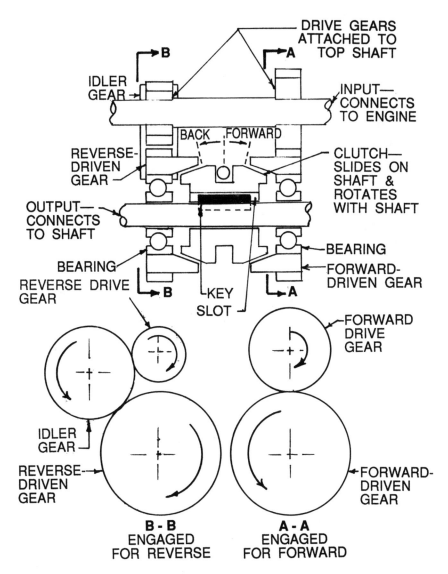

Fig. 9-6. Operation of the two-shaft transmission

permit horizontal adjustment and the upper and lower nuts provide the vertical adjustment (loosening the top nut and tightening the lower nut will raise that corner of the engine). All paint and rust must first be removed from the outer periphery of each half-coupling. Then the coupling bolts are withdrawn and the half-couplings pried apart to permit insertion of a feeler gauge.

The alignment process starts with placing a straightedge on top of the coupling to insure that both coupling halves are at the same height. If not, the engine mounts are adjusted (or shimmed if nonadjustable) as necessary until no gap is visible between a half-coupling and the straightedge when the straightedge is resting on the other half-coupling (Fig. 9-8). This procedure is repeated with the straightedge under the coupling. The straightedge is next placed at one side of the coupling and then at the other side of the coupling; the engine is moved sideways to eliminate any gap.

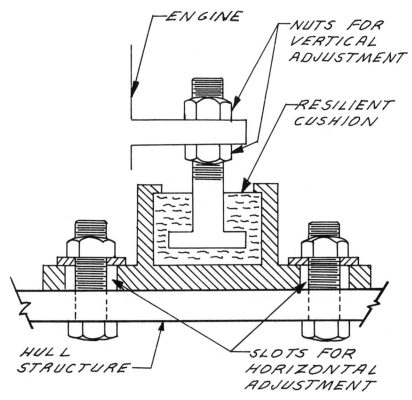

Fig. 9-7. Adjustable isolation mount

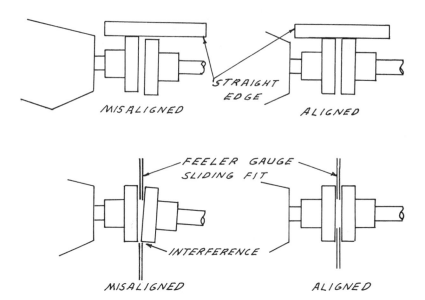

Fig. 9-8. Engine-shaft alignment. For proper alignment, all feeler gauge readings must be within three-thousandths of an inch.

After completion of the straightedge alignment, a feeler gauge is inserted between the faces of the half-couplings to insure that the faces are parallel. Feeler gauge readings are taken at the top and bottom and at each side of the gap. If the readings are all within three-thousandths of an inch, the faces can be assumed to be parallel. If not, additional adjustments must be made at the mounts until satisfactory feeler gauge readings are obtained.

The straightedge tests must then be repeated and if additional adjustment is required, the feeler gauge test must also be repeated until all tests are satisfactory without additional adjustments. The coupling bolts are then inserted and tightened.

On large vessels, the weight of the shaft will cause a significant deflection and will require a computation to determine the compensating upward force that must be applied to the end of the shaft (with a spring scale); this type of alignment is best left to professionals. Also on larger vessels, an intermediate bearing (between the coupling and the cutlass bearing) is sometimes installed. This bearing must be positioned concentric with the shaft after shaft deflection is taken into account; this is also best accomplished by professionals.

Shaft alignment must only be attempted when the boat has been waterborne for at least 24 hours (the hull takes a different shape in the water), and preferably after fuel, water, and stores are on board. Shaft alignment can be a time-consuming process but it is extremely important, as improper alignment may result in vibration of the propeller shaft, excessive wear of the cutlass bearing, and damage to the transmission oil seal.

Attachment to the Shaft

The coupling is usually attached to the propeller shaft by means of a key that fits into a slot machined into the end of the propeller shaft. The key insures that there is no rotational motion between the shaft and the hub of the coupling; however, the key does not prevent fore-and-aft movement of the shaft relative to the coupling. If the shaft is not a tight fit inside the hub of the coupling, it can withdraw from the coupling when the vessel is backing (thrust is towards the stern when backing). In an extreme condition the shaft can back all the way out of the boat, allowing water to enter through the space vacated by the shaft. To prevent this, set screws, extending into dimpled holes in the shaft, are usually inserted in the hub and safety-wired. As an added safety measure, a hose clamp may be installed about the propeller shaft to prevent the possibility of the complete loss of the propeller shaft (Fig. 9-9).

Propeller Shaft Seal

The propeller shaft seal permits free rotation of the shaft as it passes from the inside to the outside of the hull, while allowing the minimum flow of water into the hull. Two types of propeller shaft seals are presently used: the shaft seal, in which the sealing surface is the outer periphery of the rotating shaft, and the face seal, in which the sealing surface is the face of a collar attached to the rotating shaft.

The Shaft Seal

The shaft seal, otherwise known as a packing gland or stuffing box, is the most widely used, and consists of at least three rings of packing (impregnated with a lubricant) positioned about the shaft (Fig. 9-9). A packing nut compresses the packing to minimize the gap between the rotating shaft and the stationary packing. The body of the packing gland is attached with hose clamps to a shaft log (a flexible rubber hose); the other end of the shaft log is attached to the hull. This arrangement permits the packing to automatically center itself about the propeller shaft.

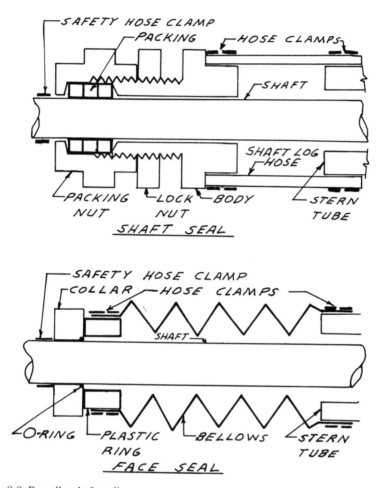

Fig. 9-9. Propeller shaft sealing

The packing nut should be tightened to allow the escape of about one or two drops of water per minute when the shaft is turning and no leakage when the engine is not being used. Excessive leakage indicates that the lubricant has leached out of the packing, causing it to become hard and brittle; it must then be replaced. It is important that the packing nut not be overtightened in an attempt to reduce excessive leakage; tightening brittle packing will score the shaft. Excessive scoring will necessitate replacement of the shaft.

The difficulty in replacing packing lies in removal of the old packing. First the locknut must be loosened and then the packing nut unthreaded. A small screwdriver or hooklike tool can be used to withdraw the packing from the packing nut. The last ring is particularly difficult to remove. New rings, of the proper cross section, must be carefully cut to an exact length so that there is no gap between the ends of the ring when the packing is wrapped around the shaft. The rings are then inserted around the shaft and pressed into the packing nut. Rings must be staggered to prevent a continuous leak path. The packing nut is then threaded onto the body but only hand tight. Repacking is best done when the boat is hauled. Final adjustment should be made after the boat is waterborne and the engine has been running with the shaft rotating for about ten minutes to permit the packing to wear in.

The Face Seal

The face seal (Fig. 9-9) consists of (1) a stainless steel collar, with an O-ring seal, that is secured to the shaft with setscrews; (2) a stationary ring, made of a noncorrosive antifriction material that contacts the collar; and (3) a bellows, one end of which is attached to the ring and the other to the stern tube. The bellows exerts a springlike force on the ring to press the stationary ring against the rotating collar. The sealing surface is between the collar and the ring.

Advantages and Disadvantages

Both the shaft seal and the face seal have advantages and disadvantages. The face seal requires no periodic adjustment and allows practically no leakage of water, but the replacement of any component requires that the coupling be removed from the shaft, usually a formidable task. The shaft seal requires intermittent tightening and periodic replacement of the packing, but this can be done without disturbing the attachment of the shaft to the coupling.

The Cutlass Bearing

The cutlass bearing (or strut bearing) supports the shaft at its after end. The bearing is usually located in a strut that is attached to the hull just forward of the propeller (Fig. 9-1). On full-keel sailboats, this shaft bearing is located in the after edge of the keel. The bearing is water lubricated and includes grooves in the bearing surface to permit the water flowing through the bearing (due to the forward motion of the vessel) to wash out any accumulated sand or silt. The life of the bearing depends on operating hours and alignment. Operation in sandy or muddy water will shorten bearing life. With the boat out of the water, bearing wear can be determined by pushing the propeller up and down and sideways. There should be little or no clearance; the bearing should grip the shaft snugly. Excessive clearance necessitates the installation of a new bearing.

Removal of the old bearing is theoretically a simple task: the bearing is held in the strut by setscrews and, after the setscrews are removed, the bearing should slide out between the bore of the strut and the shaft. However, the bearing usually becomes corroded in place and removal is difficult. Usually it is necessary to remove the propeller shaft, cut the bearing lengthwise with a hacksaw, and then pry and tap the bearing out of the strut. Removal of the shaft requires disassembly of the coupling hub from the shaft.

The Propeller

The propeller is keyed to the shaft, and the propeller nut (secured with a cotter pin) forces the tapered bore of the propeller against a mating taper on the shaft. To protect the shaft and propeller against galvanic corrosion, a sacrificial zinc split collar is bolted about the shaft adjacent to the propeller. The strut may also be protected with its own sacrificial zinc.

INBOARD/OUTBOARD DRIVE

The inboard/outboard drive arrangement (also known as in/out drive, stern drive, and out drive) consists of (1) the engine mounted inboard just forward of the transom, (2) a drive shaft arrangement that pierces the transom, and (3) a drive assembly that extends from the drive shaft into the water just aft of the transom (Fig. 9-10). The drive assembly is similar to that used on transom-mounted outboard engines. This arrangement was initially intended for use on gasoline engine–powered, high-speed, trailerable boats, but is now being used on larger boats that are diesel powered and are permanently waterborne. Some diesel-powered in/out drives are equipped with counter-rotating propellers to increase propulsion efficiency (Fig. 9-11).

The in/out drive arrangement provides the following advantages.

1. The outdrive pivots about a vertical centerline. This eliminates the need for a rudder and improves maneuverability.
2. The drive assembly can also be pivoted about a horizontal centerline, moving the propeller up and down. This permits shallow water operation and beaching.
3. There is no propeller shaft seal, as the shaft does not pierce the hull below the waterline.
4. Locating the engine adjacent to the transom provides accessible below-deck space just forward of the engine.

However, there are two basic disadvantages:

1. Normally the vessel must be out of the water to change the oil in the outdrive.
2. The Z-shaped power transmission requires many gears and bearings; repairs are costly.

THE OUTBOARD DIESEL

Transom-mount diesel outboards were introduced in Europe several years ago but were never popular in the United States because of their great weight and small horsepower. Recently, the Yanmar Diesel Engine Co., Ltd., has developed a diesel engine outboard; at the time of this writing, this product is still in the field test stage. Preliminary specifications are the following:

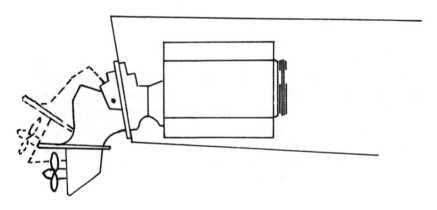

Fig. 9-10. Inboard/outboard drive

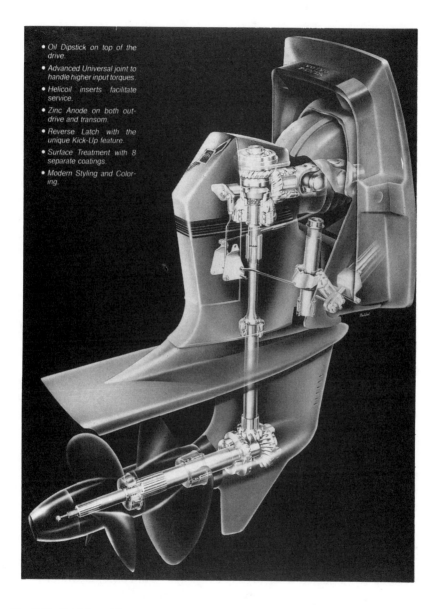

- Oil Dipstick on top of the drive.
- Advanced Universal joint to handle higher input torques.
- Helicoil inserts facilitate service.
- Zinc Anode on both out-drive and transom.
- Reverse Latch with the unique Kick-Up feature.
- Surface Treatment with 8 separate coatings.
- Modern Styling and Coloring.

Fig. 9-11. Outdrive with counter-rotating propellers for improved efficiency and performance (Courtesy Volvo North America Corp (Penta))

- 27 horsepower
- 4,500 RPM
- 3-cylinder
- 4-stroke cycle

- Overhead cam
- Weight 178.6 lbs. (81 kg)
- Raw water cooling
- Unit injectors

The lower propulsion unit is comparable to a conventional gasoline-powered outboard.

MAINTENANCE

Inboard

Transmission (and Reduction Gear)
The type of oil and the frequency of oil change is specified in the manufacturer's manual (usually every 1,000 operating hours, but at least once each season). Also, the oil should be changed if there is any evidence that it has been overheated. If the oil cannot be readily drained (Fig. 9-12), it can be pumped out with a hand pump (the same way as the engine lubricating oil).

Clutch Linkage
At least once each season the clutch linkage should be lubricated and checked for tightness of linkage and support bracket fasteners.

Transmission Oil Cooler
If seawater is circulated through the transmission oil cooler, the zincs should be checked every two months and replaced if necessary (see "Zincs" in Chapter 3).

Alignment
After a boat has been hauled, an alignment check should be conducted at least 24 hours after it is again waterborne .

Shaft Seal
Water leakage from a stuffing box should be observed frequently and the packing nut adjusted if leakage is excessive. (An abnormal water level in the bilge or frequent operation of an automatic bilge pump is usually an indication of excessive stuffing box leakage.) If adjustment does not stop excessive leakage, the packing will require replacement.

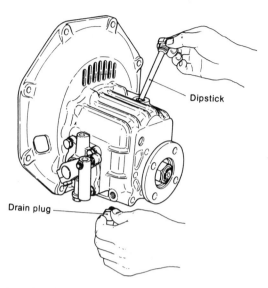

Fig. 9-12. Transmission oil drain and dipstick (Courtesy Yanmar Diesel Engine (USA), Inc.)

The frequency of repacking depends on usage; packing replacement will normally be more frequent on a powerboat than on a sailboat that seldom operates its engine. After two or three years, regardless of usage, the packing will tend to become brittle and should be replaced. Repacking when a boat is hauled for bottom painting is good preventative maintenance.

Caution: The locknut must be tightened after adjustment of the packing nut.

Caution: Overtightening brittle packing may force the packing to seize the shaft. The packing nut and body would then tend to rotate with the shaft and destroy the watertight hose clamp seals at each end of the shaft log hose. The resulting flooding could be disastrous.

Cutlass Bearing
Every time the boat is hauled, the cutlass bearing should be checked. If clearance is excessive, the bearing should be replaced.

Shaft Zinc Collar
This should be inspected about every two months to insure that the zinc is still capable of protecting the propeller and shaft. Most boat owners

arrange with a bottom cleaning service (diver) to inspect zincs and re-place when necessary.

In/Out Drive

Oil Change
The frequency of oil change is specified in the manufacturer's manual (about every six months). Also, if the drained oil appears milky, this is an indication of water leaking into the outdrive. Repair should be scheduled immediately.

Paint
Outdrives that are kept in seawater should be painted with an epoxy paint (as a barrier coat) or with a tin-based paint to protect the aluminum outdrive from the seawater.

    Caution: Do not apply a copper-base paint to an aluminum surface (it will accentuate galvanic corrosion).

Zincs
Check frequently and replace when about one-third decomposed.

Outdrive Service
Outdrives that are stored in seawater should be serviced by a professional at least once each season. This involves partial disassembly to permit inspection of the bellows and the bellows clamping arrangement. Any leakage will result in costly repairs.

CHAPTER 10

Engine Operation

THE engine operating procedures presented in this chapter are to be regarded as general guidelines and are not meant to supersede instructions specified in the manufacturer's manual, which should be studied for specific instructions and kept on board for ready reference.

INSTRUMENTATION

Engine performance can only be monitored with instruments.

Minimum Instrumentation	Preferred Instrumentation
Low oil pressure alarm	Low oil pressure alarm
	Oil pressure gauge
Water temperature gauge	Water temperature gauge
	High water temperature alarm
Ammeter	Ammeter
	Voltmeter
Fuel level gauge (or sounding rod)	Fuel level gauge (or sounding rod)
	Tachometer
	Hour meter

BEFORE STARTING THE ENGINE

1. Check engine lubricating oil level.
2. Check transmission oil level.
3. Check coolant level in expansion tank (omit for raw water cooling).
4. Check fuel supply.
5. Open fuel shutoff valve.
6. Open sea cock (omit for keel cooling).
7. Open exhaust shutoff valve (if fitted).
8. Check combustion air inlet; remove any debris and obstructions.
9. Turn main battery switch on.
10. Insure that decompression lever, if fitted, is in RUN position.

11. If manual or automatic shutdown system is installed, make sure that the air inlet baffle or control is in the OPEN position.
12. If the fuel injection pump is equipped with a STOP lever, make sure that the lever control is in the RUN position.

STARTING THE ENGINE

1. Place transmission lever into NEUTRAL (central) position.
2. Set throttle for one-third to two-thirds open.
3. Turn starter switch to ON; this will energize the electric fuel pump and/or fuel solenoid (if fitted).
4. Activate the glow plugs or combustion air preheat (if fitted). If cold weather, activate excess fuel device (if fitted).
5. Turn key to full right (START position) or push the start button. Starter will crank engine and engine should start. Release key or button immediately after engine starts; key will automatically return to ON position.

Caution: Do not crank continuously for more than 20 seconds (see Chapter 8, "The Starting System").

6. Oil pressure alarm should have stopped when engine started; if not, stop engine immediately.
7. Run engine at part throttle and no load for about five minutes.
8. Check ammeter; it should indicate CHARGE.
9. Check operation of raw water cooling pump by observing if water is being intermittently discharged from exhaust outlet. If not, stop engine (omit for keel cooling).
10. Set throttle at idle. With mooring lines still attached, check operation of power transmission system by shifting from NEUTRAL to FORWARD, to NEUTRAL, to REVERSE, to NEUTRAL.

Caution: Do not hold turbocharger compressor for any reason while engine is running; this could result in personal injury.

UNDERWAY

1. When first underway, continue at low speed until engine reaches normal operating temperature; then speed may be gradually increased.

2. Do not exceed 80 percent of maximum engine speed except for short intervals.*

3. Reduce speed to idle before shifting, then shift firmly, pausing slightly in neutral.

4. Do not race the engine (you may cause serious damage).

5. Do not put battery switch in OFF position while engine is running (see Chapter 8, "The Starting System").

6. Do not reduce speed suddenly; wake may cause backflow into exhaust piping (see Chapter 7, "The Exhaust System").

7. Avoid idling for more than 10 minutes.

8. When approaching your destination, reduce speed early to permit metal parts to cool.

Caution: On turbocharged engines, low-speed operation before stopping is required to allow time for the turbine to slow down. Stopping the engine suddenly also stops oil flow to the turbocharger, which may still be coasting at 15,000 RPM; this may result in destruction of the turbocharger bearings.

9. Monitor performance of the engine by frequent observation of instruments.

STOPPING THE ENGINE

1. Place throttle in IDLE position.

2. Place transmission shift lever in NEUTRAL (central) position.

3. Let engine operate for 3 to 5 minutes (longer for turbocharged engines; see manufacturer's manual).

4. Place throttle in STOP position or activate stop lever. Do not use decompression lever to stop engine (this will damage the exhaust valves).

5. Turn key to OFF position.

6. Open main battery switch only after engine has come to a complete stop.

---

*Most manufacturers recommend that the operator maintain a cruising (or continuous) speed of 10–15 percent less than maximum speed and some manufacturers limit maximum speed operation to a period of one to two hours. (Check the manufacurer's manual.)

7. If engine is to remain stopped for more than a day, or if vessel is
   to be unattended, close the fuel valve, sea cock, and exhaust
   valve (if fitted).

THE ENGINE LOG

The engine log is a record of all activities related to the engine and its
ancillary equipment and should be maintained by the boat operator. A
separate entry is required for each service event, every repair or component replacement, any abnormal instrument reading, every fueling
(noting the gallons received), and when lubrication oil is added (noting
the amount). Each entry should be preceded by the date and the engine
hour meter reading. Any convenient size notebook, with nonremovable
pages, can be used as a logbook.

The log will provide a ready reference to determine the time for the
next service and will point up a recurring problem or malfunction that
indicates a need for repair. Fuel consumption can readily be determined
by dividing the gallons received when fueling by the engine hours since
the last fueling.

Perhaps the greatest value of the engine log is when the boat is put
up for sale; the prospective purchaser is usually impressed by documen-
tation of the required service activities.

Winter Shutdown

IN northern areas, recreational vessels are usually decommissioned and stored out of the water for the winter period. The following steps are recommended primarily to prevent freeze damage.

1. Change lube oil and lube oil filter element. This should be done while the vessel is still in the water so that the engine can be operated to heat the oil before draining. If oil change is delayed until spring recommissioning, any acid in the oil will have attacked the bearings and journals during the winter months.
2. Close the sea cock.
3. Drain the raw water system, making sure that all low spots are thoroughly drained. This may require disassembly of hose and pipe fittings.
4. Remove the raw water pump impeller. Storage of the impeller in the pump cavity at low temperature will tend to damage the vanes and shorten the life of the impeller.
5. Loosen the V-belt adjustment so that the belt is not under tension during the winter months.
6. Check the antifreeze coolant in the freshwater cooling system with a hydrometer to insure that the coolant concentration is sufficient to withstand the lowest expected winter temperature. Add antifreeze as necessary.

    As an alternative, the freshwater system can be drained, if you make sure that all low spots are thoroughly drained. This may require disassembly of hose and pipe fittings.
7. Drain water lift muffler and seal the exhaust outlet to atmosphere.
8. Drain water out of primary fuel filter and refill through top fitting with clean fuel. It may be advisable to change the elements in the primary and secondary fuel filters at this time.
9. Remove water from bottom of fuel tank and fill tank completely to prevent atmospheric condensation. Seal the tank vent. Also, add biocide to prevent bacterial growth.

10. Remove the batteries and store them in a convenient location for periodic testing for charge with a hydrometer; keep batteries charged.
11. Make a checklist for spring recommissioning.

With the boat out of the water, it is usually a convenient time to repack the stuffing box and replace the cutlass bearing if clearance is excessive.

SPRING RECOMMISSIONING

1. Replace the raw water impeller.
2. Tighten V-belt.
3. Remove seal from fuel tank vent.
4. If freshwater system was drained, refill with coolant, making sure that all high points are vented.
5. Reinstall batteries.
6. Open sea cock.
7. Check all hose fittings for leaks.
8. Bleed air out of all high spots of raw water system.
9. Prime the raw water pump, if required.
10. Remove seal from exhaust outlet.
11. After vessel has been waterborne for at least 24 hours, check for shaft alignment; adjust as necessary.

The Engine Survey

Amarine hull survey often precedes the sale of a used boat. The buyer submits an offer through a broker to the seller; the offer is usually contingent on "a marine survey satisfactory to the buyer" and may include other conditions (e.g., sea trial, financing). If the offer is accepted, the buyer hires a marine surveyor who inspects the vessel and submits a written report regarding the vessel's material condition. If the condition of the vessel is satisfactory to the buyer, and the other conditions are met, the sale is consummated. If not, the offer is automatically cancelled unless the buyer and seller successfully negotiate the payment for the repairs that would satisfy the buyer. This system permits a buyer with little or no experience in boating to rely on the evaluation of a professional before committing for the purchase. (A current hull survey is usually required to obtain financing and insurance for a used boat.) However, the marine survey does not include an evaluation of the condition of the boat's engine(s); for this, an engine survey is required.

The engine survey is equal in importance to the hull survey and should be included as a contingency in the offer, as the hull survey is. The mechanic conducting the survey should have experience with the engine(s) to be evaluated. Unless a particular mechanic is highly recommended, the manufacturer's distributor should be contacted. Usually the distributor can conduct the survey or recommend a competent mechanic. Boatyards also can usually arrange for an engine survey.

The engine survey should be conducted in the water, before the boat is hauled for the hull survey. This permits running the engine and, if the engine survey is not satisfactory and the buyer rejects the boat, eliminates the expense of hauling the boat and conducting the hull survey.

The engine survey should include a lubricating oil analysis for each engine (see Chapter 4); even if total operating hours since the last oil change are not available, the oil analysis will provide a surprising amount of information regarding the condition of the engine.

The surveyor will usually conduct the following tests and inspections before starting the engine:

1. Check the engine lubricating oil and the transmission oil levels and look for any evidence of water in the oil.
2. Check the condition of all rubber hoses and connections.
3. Check the freshwater pump for faulty bearings.
4. Check the condition, tightness, and alignment of V-belts.
5. Observe the level of coolant in the expansion tank (a low level is usually an indication of coolant leakage).
6. Observe the freeze plugs for any sign of leakage or weeping.
7. Remove the turbocharger casing(s) to check for condition of the turbine blades and any evidence of oil leakage into the combustion air.
8. Check the compression of each cylinder by removing the injector and attaching a pressure gauge and then cranking the engine.
9. Evaluate the adequacy of the batteries, cables, and switching arrangement to provide at least one battery for engine starting and a separate battery for electrical auxiliaries.
10. Study the engine log and repair and maintenance records, if available.
11. Check for oil in the bilges and for the presence of the notice required by the U.S. Coast Guard (Chapter 4).

With the engine running, the surveyor will probably do the following:

1. Check the lubricating oil pressure with a calibrated pressure gauge (installed before the engine was started).
2. Check the adequacy of the low oil pressure alarm.
3. Check the RPM at idle with a tachometer.
4. Check the RPM at full throttle with a calibrated tachometer.
5. Check the cooling water temperature after the engine has attained its normal operating temperature.
6. Listen for knocks and any unusual noise.
7. Observe operation of all instruments.
8. Look for leaks in the lube oil, fuel oil, raw water, freshwater, and exhaust systems.
9. With the pressure cap removed from the expansion tank, look for pulsations of the freshwater level that may indicate a leaking cylinder head gasket or a cracked head.
10. With the mooring lines attached and the engine at idle, shift the transmission lever to evaluate performance of the transmission.

The cost of an engine survey usually amounts to about two hours of a mechanic's time plus the cost of the lubricating oil analysis. This is a low price to pay for the knowledge gained regarding the condition of the engine and it is well worth the investment.

Initial Maintenance on a Used Engine

EVEN if the engine log of the used boat records oil changes, filter replacement, and other maintenance items, it is best to remove all doubt about the adequacy of previous maintenance by performing the following maintenance tasks.

1. Change the engine lubricating oil.
2. Change the transmission oil.
3. Replace the primary fuel oil filter element, secondary fuel oil filter element, and lubricating oil filter element.
4. Replace the combustion air cleaner element.
5. Replace the coolant in the freshwater cooling system.
6. Clean the raw water strainer.
7. Make sure that the vacuum breaker valve or vent line is unclogged (if fitted).
8. Replace all zincs in the raw water system.
9. Remove the raw water pump impeller, inspect, and replace if necessary.
10. Check the V-belt. Replace if necessary and adjust for proper tension.
11. Drain fuel tank; fill with new fuel and add biocide.
12. Check batteries for electrolyte level and charge; recharge batteries if necessary.
13. Check all battery cables for tightness.
14. Check fire extinguishers to insure that they have been recharged within the past twelve months.
15. Clean bilges so that they are free of oil.
16. Check shaft alignment.
17. Repack stuffing box.

If the items on the following list are not in place, arrange for their installation.

1. Water-absorbing fuel oil filter.
2. Hour meter.
3. Tachometer (a tachometer wired to the alternator is not an expensive retrofit).
4. Notice required by the U.S. Coast Guard regarding prohibition of pumping oil overboard (Chapter 4).
5. Automatic Halon fire extinguisher.
6. Carbon monoxide sensor with alarm at each helm station.
7. A separate battery for engine starting and for electrical auxiliaries.

In addition, the new owner should:

1. Make sure that manufacturer's manual is on board.
2. Start an engine log.
3. Purchase the tools necessary to perform maintenance tasks and store them on board.
4. Purchase the required spare parts and engine supplies and keep them on board.
5. Practice bleeding the fuel system until proficient.

Troubleshooting Guide

Problem: Engine will not crank.

Possible cause:
- Low battery charge
- Defective wiring
- Loose or corroded electrical connection
- Waterlogged muffler
- Restriction in exhaust piping
- Defective starter motor

Problem: Engine will crank but will not start.

Possible cause:
- Throttle or stop lever in STOP position
- Fuel tank empty
- Fuel line clogged
- Primary fuel filter clogged
- Throttle linkage improperly adjusted
- Fuel pump strainer clogged
- Fuel shutoff valve closed
- Secondary fuel filter clogged
- Fuel tank vent clogged
- Air in fuel line
- Defective fuel pump solenoid
- Combustion air inlet clogged
- Defective fuel lift pump
- Combustion air cleaner clogged
- Defective fuel injection pump
- Defective or inoperable starting aid (glow plug, air preheat)
- Defective injectors
- Incorrect fuel pump timing

- Low compression
- Incorrect grade of fuel

Problem: Lack of power

Possible cause:
- Defective fuel lift pump
- Partially blocked fuel line
- Air in fuel system
- Partially clogged fuel filter (primary and/or secondary)
- Defective fuel injection pump
- Defective injectors
- Partially clogged fuel lift pump strainer
- Low compression
- Incorrect fuel pump timing
- Partially clogged fuel tank vent
- Incorrect valve timing
- Partially clogged air filter
- Improperly adjusted throttle linkage
- Restriction in combustion air supply
- Restriction in exhaust piping
- Leaking cylinder head gasket
- Kelp or foreign matter on keel
- Overheating

Problem: Overheating

Possible cause:
- Restriction in exhaust piping
- Clogged raw water strainer
- Low coolant level
- Defective raw water pump
- Defective fresh water pump
- Restriction in cooling water piping or fittings
- Leaking cylinder head gasket
- Restriction in water jacket
- Clogged heat exchanger
- Sea cock closed
- Loose water pump drive belt
- Defective thermostat

Problem: Low lubricating oil pressure

Possible cause:
- Defective oil pressure gauge
- Low oil level
- Defective oil pump
- Incorrect grade of oil
- Oil pressure relief valve stuck open
- Worn bearings
- Defective oil pressure relief valve
- Clogged oil pump strainer

Problem: Excessive smoke in exhaust

Possible cause:
- Defective air preheat system
- Overload
- Incorrect fuel pump timing
- Restricted air inlet
- Incorrect valve timing
- Air filter clogged
- Poor compression
- Defective injector(s)
- Leaking cylinder head gasket
- Defective fuel injection pump
- Lubricating oil leakage into combustion air
- Incorrect type of fuel
- Abnormally low engine temperature

Problem: Excessive fuel consumption

Possible cause:
- Defective fuel injection pump
- Clogged combustion air cleaner
- Defective injectors
- Clogged air inlet
- Incorrect fuel injection pump timing
- Restricted exhaust piping
- Incorrect type of fuel
- Incorrect valve timing

- Abnormally low engine temperature
- Poor compression

Problem: Knocking

Possible cause:
- Incorrect fuel injection pump timing
- Air in fuel line
- Overheating
- Broken valve spring
- Worn or defective bearings
- Incorrect tappet setting
- Incorrect type of lubricating oil
- Sticking valve(s)
- Lubricating oil overheated
- Low lubricating oil level

Tools

A diesel engine is a valuable piece of equipment; it should not be damaged by the use of improper tools. Compared to the cost of the engine, the purchase of the proper tools is a small investment that will reduce the time required to perform routine maintenance. For repair and overhaul, special tools are required; some of these tools are only provided by the engine manufacturer (e.g., injector removal tool). For routine maintenance the following tools are recommended:

1. Box end wrench set (Fig. E-1)
2. Open end wrench set (Fig. E-1)
3. Socket wrench set, with ratchet handle and extensions (Fig. E-1)
4. Allen head wrench set
5. Oil filter strap wrench
6. Retainer ring pliers (for raw water pump impeller)

Important: Make sure that the tips of the pliers fit the holes in the retainer ring.

7. Screwdriver set
8. Feeler gauge
9. Straightedge

Wrenches are available in metric (millimeter) and English (fractions of an inch) sizes. The engine must first be examined to determine the type and size of wrenches required (most foreign-made engines, except English, are metric). If a foreign-made engine is equipped with American-made components, both metric and English sizes will probably be required. The distance across the flats of the hexagon determines the wrench size.

Adjustable end wrenches (crescent), vise grips, and channel lock pliers (Fig. E-2) should never be used on the engine or the engine's

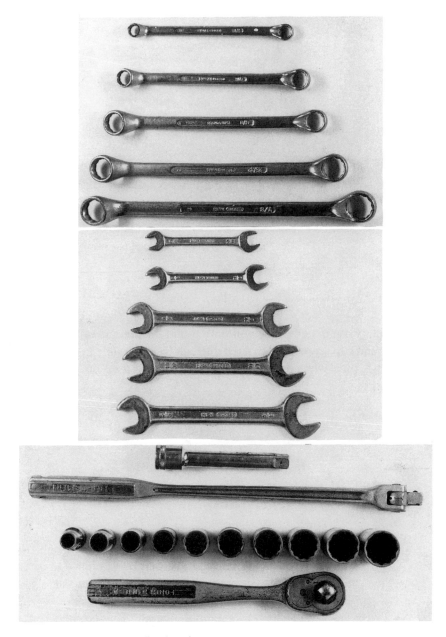

Fig. E-1. Wrenches for use on diesel engines

Fig. E-2. Wrenches *not* to be used on diesel engines

ancillary equipment; they will only round the corners of the hexagonal nuts and cap screws and make it difficult or impossible to use the proper tool. A pipe wrench (Stillson) should only be used on pipe and pipe fittings.

Spare Parts

F OR coastal cruising in local waters the following minimum inventory of spare parts and supplies is recommended.

1. Biocide, to add to fuel when refueling.
2. Lubricating oil, at least one quart.
3. Primary fuel oil filter element.
4. V-belt.
5. Raw water pump impeller and gasket.
6. Thermostat.
7. Duct tape and hose clamps (for temporary patching of water hose).

For extended cruising, the following inventory of spare parts and supplies is recommended.

1. Biocide, to add to fuel oil when refueling.
2. Lubricating oil, enough for several oil changes.
3. Transmission oil, enough for several changes.
4. Lubricating oil filter elements.
5. Primary fuel oil filter elements.
6. Fuel lift pump, or replacement diaphragm and screen.
7. Secondary fuel filter elements.
8. Combustion air cleaner elements.
9. V-belts.
10. Raw water pump impeller and gasket.
11. Freshwater pump.
12. Coolant (antifreeze).
13. Thermostat.
14. Fuel injector(s) and injector removal tool.
15. Fuel injection pump.
16. High-pressure fuel line(s).
17. Fuel line hose and fittings.

18. Water hose and hose clamps.
19. Starter.
20. Generator.
21. Starter solenoid.
22. Electrical kit, consisting of wire stripper, wire, and connectors.
23. Zincs, all sizes required.

Index